TRANSCRIPT EXERCISES

FOR

LEARNING EVIDENCE

BY

PAUL BERGMAN
Professor of Law, University of California, Los Angeles

WEST PUBLISHING CO.
ST. PAUL, MINN.
1992

Copyright © 1992

by

West Publishing Co.

All Rights Reserved

ISBN 0-314-01143-9

To my children, Kevin and Hilary.

Table of Contents

	Page
Introduction	1

Chapter 1: Competence

    <u>Transcript 1</u> ("The Oath")
        A. <u>Background</u>   4
        B. <u>Testimony</u> (<u>State v. Gillig</u>)   5

    <u>Transcript 2</u> ("Personal Knowledge")
        A. <u>Background</u>   9
        B. <u>Testimony</u> (<u>State v. Gillig cont.</u>)   9

    <u>Transcript 3</u> ("Questioning Techniques")
        A. <u>Background</u>   12
        B. <u>Testimony</u> (<u>Huston v. Dobbs</u>)   12

Chapter 2: Relevance

    <u>Transcript 4</u>
        A. <u>Background</u>   16
        B. <u>Testimony</u> (<u>O'Hare v. Hutchinson</u>)   17

    <u>Transcript 5</u>
        A. <u>Background</u>   26
        B. <u>Testimony</u> (<u>State v. Pinsky</u>)   26

Chapter 3: Hearsay

    <u>Transcript 6</u>
        A. <u>Background</u>   32
        B. <u>Testimony</u> (<u>Estate-J. Paul Giddy</u>)   33

    <u>Transcript 7</u>
        A. <u>Background</u>   39
        B. <u>Testimony</u> (<u>Keaton v. Brooks</u>)   39

    <u>Transcript 8</u>
        A. <u>Background</u>   44
        B. <u>Testimony</u> (<u>State v. Dunne</u>)   44

Chapter 4: <u>Hearsay Exceptions Not Requiring Unavailability</u>

Transcript 9 ("Admissions and Business Records")
    A. Background   53
    B. Testimony (Palmer v. Dunbar)   54

Transcript 10 ("Vicarious Admissions")
    A. Background   62
    B. Testimony
      (Palmer v. Dunbar cont.)   62

Chapter 5: Hearsay Exceptions Requiring Unavailability

Transcript 11
    A. Background   73
    B. Testimony (State v. Milhouse)   75

Chapter 6: Character Evidence

Transcript 12 ("Character to Prove Conduct")
    A. Background   90
    B. Testimony
      (Mentry v. McSoftware Corp.)   93

Transcript 13 ("Character to Prove Conduct")
    A. Background   100
    B. Testimony (State v. Edwards)   100

Transcript 14 ("Character To Impeach")
    A. Background   114
    B. Testimony (State v. Relph)   115

Chapter 7: Impeachment

Transcript 15 ("Prior Statements")
    A. Background   124
    B. Testimony
      (In the Matter of Kurt C.)   125

Transcript 16 ("Contradiction, Bias and Other Methods of Attacking Credibility")
    A. Background   136
    B. Testimony
      (Hawthorne v. Telstar Pictures)   137

Chapter 8: Examining Forgetful Witnesses

Transcript 17

	A.	Background	148
	B.	Testimony	
		(O'Hare v. Hutchinson cont.)	148

Chapter 9: Expert Testimony

Transcript 18
- A. Background — 157
- B. Testimony
  (Widower v. Atlas Ins.) — 159

Chapter 10: A Final Transcript

Transcript 19
    Testimony
    (In the Matter of Turney) — 180

Appendix: Answer Key

Transcript 1	201
Transcript 2	203
Transcript 3	205
Transcript 4	208
Transcript 5	213
Transcript 6	216
Transcript 7	218
Transcript 8	221
Transcript 9	225
Transcript 10	229
Transcript 11	234
Transcript 12	238
Transcript 13	241
Transcript 14	245
Transcript 15	251
Transcript 16	254
Transcript 17	258
Transcript 18	261
Transcript 19	267

Introduction

Despite a plethora of excellent Evidence coursebooks, both of the casebook and problem variety, students who have taken an Evidence course are often uncertain about how to apply evidence rules in real or simulated trial settings. This is ironic, because evidentiary principles developed out of the particular format of Anglo-American trials, and many of those principles can have meaning only in the context of that format.

The purpose of this text is to narrow the "theory and practice" gap by allowing you to analyze and apply many of the rules of evidence in their "natural habitat," question and answer dialogues. The transcripts are not intended to serve as the focal point of a course in Evidence. Thus, the book contains minimal exposition of evidentiary principles. Instead, it assumes that you have encountered those principles elsewhere, but need and want experience in their application.

In addition to providing something of a realistic setting for evidentiary analysis, transcripts may also help you realize that evidentiary issues often do not arise in isolation. Typically, an appellate case is selected for its ability to illustrate a particular evidentiary issue, such as "hearsay." Even problems tend to have a similar concentration. In a transcript format, as in actual trials, a single transcript can economically raise issues both of form and substance, and a variety of substantive evidentiary issues can occur in close proximity to each other. Among other advantages, the economy of space enables similar problems to arise in different contexts over the run of the book, enhancing learning by allowing you to periodically review principles previously studied.

A couple of important disclaimers. First, despite the transcript format, the focus of the materials is on rules of evidence, not the art of trial advocacy. Thus, you are asked to examine the dialogues for their compliance with evidentiary doctrine, not for their overall persuasiveness. Similarly, you should concern yourself primarily with whether a portion of a transcript is objectionable, not with whether it would make sense from an advocacy standpoint actually to make the objection.

Second, because the materials are limited to the evidentiary issues that can most profitably be explored in transcript format, the transcripts make no pretense to covering the full spectrum of evidentiary issues that you are likely to encounter in an evidence course. For example, issues such as presumptions and privilege are just as easily illustrated in appellate cases or problems as in transcripts, and they are not touched upon in the transcripts.

Using the Materials

When you examine the transcripts, you will note that only some of the questions, answers, objections, trial court rulings, and the like are numbered. The numbered portions of a transcript are the only ones to which you are to respond. However, you cannot limit your attention to those numbered portions; typically, evidence or rulings preceding a numbered portion must be considered to gauge the propriety of a given question, answer, objection or ruling.

You will be required to make a number of types of response. If a question or answer is numbered, you will have to formulate for yourself the objection that might be available. Formulate any reasonable objection, and then state whether in the context of the particular case it is likely to be sustained.

If a ruling or an objection is numbered, your task is to state whether that particular ruling or objection is correct and, if not, whether some other one would be.

Most important, you are to ignore the "waiver" rule. Normally, if counsel fails to make a timely objection, any objection may be deemed waived, and the trial judge's failure to keep out testimony on her or his own will not be reviewed on appeal. In the transcripts that follow, often there is no objection or ruling that "flags" a potential evidentiary issue. This is entirely realistic. In actual trials, you must pick up the evidentiary signals on your own; no one stops the testimony to ask you if a particular rules applies. Do not simply state something like, "Well, since no objection was made, it's been waived, so the issue is moot." Instead, state what objection, if any, would have been available. If you conclude that no objection would have been available, identify the evidentiary principle that supports your conclusion.

Finally, an Appendix at the back of the book consists of my suggested responses to each numbered portion of a transcript. Therefore, you may use the transcripts as a personal study aid. You may, however, want to add to the realism by doing at least some of the transcripts orally, perhaps in a study group or classroom exercise. For more so in Evidence that in other law school courses, you must train you ear as well as your eye to recognize evidentiary issues.

The transcripts are entirely fictional, and no reference to any real person, dead or living, or to Kenny Hegland, is intended. Unless I am out to get somebody.

Chapter 1

Competence

Transcript 1: "The Oath" (FRE 104, 603)

A. Background

Every witness begins testifying by taking an oath (or affirmation) to tell the truth. Usually, the witness' ability to understand what it means to tell the truth is assumed. No inquiry into a witness' ability to distinguish lying from truthtelling is made, either by a judge or by the party calling the witness. In the unusual instance in which opposing counsel believes a witness may not understand the duty to be truthful, opposing counsel must object and ask to take the witness on "voir dire" for the purpose of inquiring into the witness' understanding of the oath.

An exception to the usually uninterrupted flow from oath to testimony occurs when a witness' understanding of the duty to be truthful cannot be assumed. When a witness is a young child, or is suffering from certain mental infirmities, the party calling the witness often must intercede after the oath is administered to make an affirmative showing that the witness can distinguish a lie from the truth, and understands the duty to be truthful.

"Mini-trials" As we know, pessimists view partially filled glasses of water as half empty, whereas optimists view them as half full. Pessimists who stop staring at glasses of water long enough to attend law school probably view the Federal Rules of Evidence as a catalog of exclusionary rules, while optimists are likely to understand the rules as a set of foundations that must be shown before certain evidence can be admitted.

The rules frequently validate the optimists' view; many of them operate less as bars and more as foundational rules to admissibility. Sometimes, a dispute arises as to the sufficiency of a foundation. For example, a party may contend that a lay witness lacks competence, that the conditions for the "excited utterance" hearsay exception do not exist, or that a purported expert is unqualified. In such situations, a "mini-trial" typically occurs. In the mini-trial, parties offer evidence to prove or disprove foundational elements free of the rules of evidence. (FRE 104) The proponent of evidence normally has the burden of persuading the judge that the foundation is adequate. (FRE 104 (a)) On occasion, however, the proponent can succeed even if the judge is not convinced of the foundation's adequacy, as long as the jury could reasonably believe that the foundation is adequate. (FRE 104 (b))

B. <u>Testimony</u>

<u>State v. David Gillig</u>

Prosecution for sexual abuse of minor children at the Happy Daze Pre-School. The defendant is the owner of and a teacher at the school. The prosecution contends that over a period of 18 months, the defendant (among others) involved children in illegal sexual activity, and threatened the children with harm if they told anyone about it. The defense is a denial that sexual acts of any nature ever took place. As its first witness, the prosecution calls Jimmy Jones, a former Happy Daze student. When Jimmy arrives at the witness chair, the court clerk asks him to raise his right hand. The clerk then asks, "Do you swear that the testimony you will give will be the truth, the whole truth, and nothing but the truth?" Jimmy answers, "Yes," and sits down. The following then takes place.

<u>Direct Examination by Prosecution</u>

Q: Jimmy, what is your name?

A: Jimmy Jones.

Q: And how old are you, Jimmy?

1. A: I'm six years old. My birthday is March 31.

2. Q: All right, Jimmy. I know this courtroom seems big and maybe a little scary, but we're your friends here and I want you to relax and tell us what happened to you, just like when you did when I talked to you in my office. Is that OK?

    A: OK.

    Q: Jimmy, let's go back...

    Def. Att: Excuse the interruption, counsel. Your Honor, before the witness starts testifying, I request permission to ask a few foundational questions going to his qualifications.

    The Court: What aspect of his qualifications do you intend to pursue?

    Def. Att: The witness' ability to understand the oath, Your Honor.

3. The Court: I'll allow the inquiry. However, since the prosecution has the burden of establishing that the witness is qualified, the prosecutor shall begin the foundational inquiry.

4. The Court: We'll conduct the hearing before the jury, as information relating to competency issues is unlikely to prejudice the defendant should I ultimately decide that the witness is not competent. However, I'll consider either counsel's request to excuse the jury during the voir dire examination should it become necessary. Counsel, you may inquire.

<u>Voir Dire Examination by Prosecution</u>

Q: Jimmy, what if I told you that my suit is orange, with purple and green stripes, would that be the truth or a lie?

A: The truth.

Q: That's right, very good. And what if I told you that it is nighttime right now?

A: That's not true.

Q: If I were to tell you that Santa Claus is not real, but merely the merchandising creation of a materialistic world, would that be the truth?

A: (No response; witness sobbing.)

Q: Well, I'll ask another question. Do bad things happen to you if you don't tell the truth?

A: Yeah, my mommy and daddy get mad at me.

Q: What happens when they get mad at you?

A: Sometimes I have to go to my room, or I get a spanking.

Q: That person over there (indicating the clerk) gave you an oath. Do you know what that means?

A: It means I have to tell the truth.

Q: Will you tell the truth today?

A: Yes.

Pros: No further questions, Your Honor.

The Court: Defense counsel may inquire.

Voir Dire Examination by Defense Counsel

Q: Jimmy, do you always tell the truth?

A: I guess not.

Q: So sometimes you tell a lie?

A: Uh-huh (witness nods head up and down).

Q: Sometimes when you lie, is it so you won't get into trouble?

A: I guess so.

Q: And sometimes you might tell a lie about someone because you don't like them?

A: I don't know. Maybe.

Q: You don't like Mr. Gillig, do you, Jimmy?

A: I don't like him anymore.

Q: Jimmy, do you think you might lie to punish Mr. Gillig?

A: I don't know.

Def. Att: Nothing further, Your Honor.

The Court: Anything further from the prosecution?

Redirect Voir Dire Examination by Prosecution

Q: Just one question. Jimmy, is what you are going to tell us the truth?

5. A: Yes, it's just like I told that lady before, he was always touching my privates.

Pros: Nothing further.

6. The Court: I find beyond a reasonable doubt that Jimmy is competent to testify. Prosecution may resume questioning.

Q (Pros): OK, Jimmy, now let's go back...

Transcript 2: "Personal Knowledge" (FRE 602)

A. Background

In addition to understanding the oath, every witness (or at least, every non-expert witness) must be "percipient;" that is, a witness' testimony must be based on personal knowledge. A witness must have personally seen, heard, tasted, touched or smelled whatever the witness is testifying about.

A witness' personal knowledge is generally established through the witness' own testimony. This is sensible. Consider the difficulties if one had to call Witness # 2 to testify to the personal knowledge of Witness # 1. One would first have to call Witness # 3 to testify to Witness # 2's personal knowledge. But first...

B. Testimony

State v. David Gillig (cont.)

Following the judge's ruling above, the prosecution began its questioning of Jimmy. Below is an excerpt from that questioning.

Direct Examination by Prosecution

    Q: Jimmy, do you remember the day that Mr. Gillig took some pictures of you when you weren't wearing any clothes?

1. A: I think so.

    Q: Before he took the pictures, did he say anything to you about why he wanted to take your picture?

    A: Yeah.

    Q: Can you tell us as closely as you can just what he said to you?

2. A: I don't remember exactly, something about so the school doctor could examine me better.

3. Q: What do you think was his real reason?

A: My daddy says he was sick in the head.

Q: Where did Mr. Gillig take these pictures?

A: In his office.

Q: How did you happen to go to his office?

A: I was playing, and a teacher told me to go there.

Q: Which teacher was it?

4. A: I think it was Mrs. White, one of the new teachers, but I'm not sure.

Q: Do you remember how she looked when she told you this?

A: She was smiling.

5. Q: Jimmy, you know that sometimes people smile when they don't really mean it. Do you think this was one of those "I don't really mean it" smiles?

A: Yeah, maybe.

Q: Now, how many pictures did he take?

6. A: I don't know. I guess 10 or 15.

Q: Did he touch you at all?

A: I don't know. Maybe.

7. Q: Might he have touched your privates?

A: I don't remember.

Q: How long were you in his office?

A: I can't remember exactly.

8. Q: Can you give us an estimate, some idea of how long it was?

A: I think it was about...

Cross Examination by Defense Counsel

Q: Do you remember what day of the week it was that you say Mr. Gillig took pictures of you when you weren't wearing clothes?

A: I don't know, a schoolday I guess.

Q: How about the time of day?

A: I don't know.

Q: Can you describe the kind of camera he was using?

A: No.

Q: You don't really remember very much about the incident at all, do you Jimmy?

A: I guess not.

Def. Att: Your Honor, I move to strike all of this witness' testimony relating to the alleged taking of photographs, on the ground that he lacks personal knowledge.

9. The Court: The issue is whether there is sufficient evidence for the jury to conclude reasonably that he has personal knowledge.

10. The Court: What ruling on the motion?

Transcript 3: Questioning Techniques (FRE 611)

A. Background

Unlike the Internal Revenue Code, which began and largely defines people's tax liabilities, the Federal Rules of Evidence are an overlay on trial processes that were hundreds of years old before the rules came along. Many of these processes simply went uncodified. For example, no rule governs the sequence of presentation of evidence at trial. However, the sequence is largely unchanging and unquestioned. (An ancient scholar probably said the same thing about "trial by battle" in 1172!)

Similarly, apart from provisions in Rule 611 (c) regarding leading questions, the manner in which judges permit attorneys to question witnesses is not codified, and is left largely to the control and discretion of the court. Nevertheless, the contours of that discretion are reasonably clear. A question should be understandable, and it should seek information as opposed to asking a witness merely to confirm information contained in the question. A question should be reasonably limited in scope, so that both a witness and opposing counsel know what information is sought. (Otherwise, the latter may be unable to interpose an appropriate objection. Think of the difficulty posed by an overbroad question such as, "Please tell us what you think we ought to know about what happened.") On the negative side, counsel should avoid arguing with a witness, and using the power to ask questions as an excuse to make statements or insert information into the record.

B. Testimony

Huston v. Dobbs

Civil suit for damages for alleged misrepresentations made by Dobbs, a travel agent, to Huston. Huston claims damages arising from Dobbs' false statements concerning the luxurious amenities of a resort hotel in the Sierra Madre Mountains in Mexico. In the transcript excerpt below, Huston is testifying to conditions at the hotel.

<u>Direct Examination by Plaintiff's Counsel</u>

1. Q: Ms. Huston, please describe the condition of the hotel in your own words.

2. A: It was really a mess, far and away the worst hellhole I have ever stayed in.

3. Q: Did you actually see rats in your room?

   A: Yes, just about every day.

4. Q: Please tell us about the first time you noticed the rats.

5. A: I'll never forget it. On the first day I arrived, I was getting ready to take a van tour of the area. I had unpacked my suitcase and started to put it away under the bed. Suddenly this big rat came running out from under the bed and ran across the room. Then a few seconds later another rat ran out from under the bed too. Obviously the hotel knew about the rat problem.

6. Q: You testified that the rats ran across the room. Did you see where they went?

   A: They disappeared into a hole in a corner of the room.

7. Q: Let me turn your attention to the hotel's parasailing program. Do you recall that aspect of the trip?

   A: I certainly do.

   Q: What if anything had Mr. Dobbs told you about the program?

   A: He said that it was one of the best programs of its kind anywhere. He told me that all instructors were licensed, that the equipment was always state-of-the-art and constantly maintained, that the hotel supplied all the equipment, and that the cost of lessons and two parasails per day was included in the price of the vacation.

8. Q: What was the program like in actuality? Was the cost of parasailing in fact included in the vacation price?

   A: No. An hour lesson was $60, and anytime after that that I wanted to parasail was $15.

9. Q: When you would complain to the hotel manager that you thought you had already paid for parasailing, how did the manager respond?

10. A: She just kept saying she was sorry, but that had never been hotel policy. Let me add, too, that the instructors were just people they would get off the beach--there were always different people there, and most of the time they didn't even know where the equipment was kept.

11. Q: What happened next?

    A: Well, the equipment wasn't very good either. A couple of times they couldn't even get the boat started.

    Q: Turning next...

Cross Examination by Defense Counsel

12. Q: Ms. Huston, isn't it a fact that Mr. Dobbs told you that he had no information about the hotel's parasailing program?

13. A: That's not true, he's lying if he says that.

14. Q: If anyone's the liar, isn't it you?

    A: No.

    Q: Why would Mr. Dobbs have made all these misstatements to you?

15. A: He had told me that business was pretty slow. I suspect that he figured he could make some easy money by making this trip seem like a great bargain.

    Q: You lost your job shortly after returning from the holiday, did you not?

    A: Yes. But let me explain...

16. Q: Excuse me, but you've answered my question. Your attorney can question you further if she so desires. Nothing further at this time, Your Honor.

Chapter 2

Relevance

Transcript 4 (FRE 401, 402, 403)

A. **Background**

"Relevance" refers to the tendency of a proffered item of evidence to make an element of applicable substantive law more or less probable than it would be without the item of evidence. A proffered item's relevance may derive either from its factual connection to a legal element, or from its relationship to the credibility of a witness. Relevance issues are not decided by principles of abstract logical reasoning, but by ordinary life experiences.

Evidence is either direct or circumstantial; by definition, relevance concerns arise only when evidence is circumstantial. For example, assume that Ray is on trial for armed robbery of a convenience store; the element of substantive law which the prosecution seeks to establish is "identity of the perpetrator." Randy testifies, "That guy over there (pointing to Ray) was the robber." This is direct evidence; no inference (other than the accuracy of Randy's testimony) is necessary to link the evidence to the element. By definition, the evidence is relevant.

Assume next that in the same case, also to establish the element, "identity of the perpetrator," Julie testifies, "I saw Ray in the store two days before the robbery." This is circumstantial evidence; the testimony links up to the element only by means of an inference. Here, the inference would depend on generalizations along the lines of, "People who are in a store two days before it is robbed are sometimes there to case it;" and "People who case a store sometimes rob it." While the prosecution would concede that these generalizations are less than universally accurate, experience suggests that they are true often enough to have a "tendency" to make the element of "identity" more probable than it would be without the evidence. Thus, the evidence is relevant.

Finally, again in the same case, assume that on the defendant's behalf, to disprove the element, "identity of the perpetrator", Matthew testifies, "Ray's and Julie's relationship came to a stormy ending two weeks before the robbery." Here, no factual linkage between the evidence and the element exists. But experience suggests that people whose relationships have had stormy endings sometimes harbor angry grudges towards their ex-lovers, and that people who harbor angry grudges sometimes testify falsely. Thus, the evidence provides relevant circumstantial evidence as to Julie's credibility.

The test of relevance is a minimal one. In earlier days, judges wanting to exclude evidence sometimes had to artificially raise the threshold of relevance. Under Federal Rule 403, judges can straightforwardly reject relevant evidence if its probative value is outweighed by the dangers of unfair prejudice or confusion, or by considerations of undue delay.

B. <u>Testimony</u>

<u>O'Hare v. Hutchinson</u>

Civil suit for damages for personal injuries suffered by O'Hare as a result of having been struck on September 22 by a car driven by Hutchinson. O'Hare claims that he was in a crosswalk at the intersection of Main and Peach Streets when Hutchinson negligently made a left turn into Main, striking and injuring O'Hare. During O'Hare's case-in-chief, O'Hare called a witness who testified that she observed what happened because she was stopped on Main waiting for the light to change to green. She testified that Hutchinson was traveling along Peach at 30-35 m.p.h., that Hutchinson did not slow down as she made a left turn onto Main, that she appeared to be looking at something on the seat next to her rather than at the street, and that Hutchinson struck O'Hare in the crosswalk. O'Hare also testified that he was in the crosswalk when struck. Hutchinson contends that she was driving carefully, and that O'Hare was struck not in the crosswalk, but about 25 yards up the block when he suddenly ran out from between two parked cars.

Below is a portion of the examination of defendant Hutchinson.

<u>Direct Examination by Defense Counsel</u>

1. Q: Ms. Hutchinson, how are you employed?

    A: I'm a building contractor.

    Q: How long have you been a contractor?

    A: For about 12 years now.

2. Q: Have you worked on any well-known projects?

3. A: Well, I'm proud to say that the Sewer Sludge Reclamation Plant was my project. And a couple of years ago, I received our industry's customer satisfaction award.

    Q: All right, let me turn your attention to the events of September 22, at about 3:00 in the afternoon. What were you doing at about that time?

    A: I was on my way to a construction project over on Main and 3rd, about 6 blocks away from where the accident took place.

    Q: Where were you coming from?

    A: A small remodeling job over on Elm, a couple of miles away.

    Q: What type of vehicle were you travelling in?

    A: A company pickup truck.

4. Q: What route did you take to get to Main & 3rd?

	A:	The most direct route, up Elm to Peach, then it's about a mile over to Main.
5.	Q:	How fast do you usually drive when you're going from one job to another?
	A:	No more than 30 m.p.h. in the city.
6.	Q:	30 m.p.h. Now, as you drove up Elm in the direction of Peach, approximately what speed were you going?
	A:	No more than 20 m.p.h.
7.	Q:	Was there any particular reason that you were driving 20 m.p.h. on this occasion?
	A:	Yes. I had picked up expensive kitchen cabinets earlier in the day, and though they were tied down I did not want to bump them.
8.	Q:	In the year prior to this incident, about how many times per month would you say you drove through the intersection of Peach and Main?
	A:	On the average, at least 8-10 times.
9.	Q:	Please describe what happened as you were driving along Peach and approached Main.
	A:	I went into the left turn lane and slowed down to turn left. I made the turn onto Main, and had straightened out and was starting to pick up a bit of speed when suddenly he [pointing to O'Hare] ran into the street. I never saw him until then. I tried to stop and swerve, but it was too late.
10.	Q:	So you at no time saw Mr. O'Hare in the crosswalk?
	A:	No.

Q: Have you ever seen Mr. O'Hare in the vicinity of Peach and Main before?

A: I'm pretty sure I have.

Q: What happened on that occasion?

Pl. Att: Your Honor, I ask permission for brief voir dire going to the witness' personal knowledge.

The Court: Be very brief.

Pl. Att: I also ask that the jury be excused for the voir dire.

11. The Court: Counsel, I see no need to take the time to excuse the jury. Please proceed.

<u>Voir Dire Examination by Plaintiff's Attorney</u>

Q: Ms. Hutchinson, on this earlier occasion that you may have seen Mr. O'Hare in the vicinity of Peach and Main, about how far away from him would you say you were?

A: I'd say about 50 feet.

Q: And as of that time, you had never seen Mr. O'Hare before, correct?

A: As far as I know, that's right.

Q: And you saw him only from the side, isn't that correct?

A: That's true.

Q: And you can't be certain it was Mr. O'Hare who you saw, can you?

A: No, but from seeing him run out from between the cars, I think it was him I saw earlier.

Pl. Att: Your Honor, I object to any testimony as to the earlier incident based on lack of personal knowledge.

The witness is simply creating an earlier incident based on the later one.

12. The Court: I merely have to decide whether the jurors could reasonably believe that the witness had personal knowledge. Based on the testimony, I'll overrule your objection. Defense counsel may proceed.

Direct Examination by Defense Counsel

Q: Ms. Hutchinson, what happened on that occasion?

A: Well, it was about a week before the accident. I was coming out of the little market on Main just north of the intersection with Peach. I saw a man crossing Main at just about the same spot that O'Hare ran out from between the two cars. I'm pretty sure the man I saw was O'Hare.

Pl. Att: Objection, Your Honor, irrelevant and unduly prejudicial under Rule 403. Move to strike.

The Court: Will both counsel approach the bench. (At the bench) Plaintiff's counsel, on what basis do you claim the testimony is irrelevant?

Pl. Att: Your Honor, there is just no connection between Mr. O'Hare allegedly having crossed Main away from the crosswalk one week earlier, and his having done so on the date he was struck.

The Court: Defense counsel, any response?

Def. Att: Your Honor, we offer the evidence of the earlier incident not to prove that O'Hare failed to use the crosswalk on the date in question. Rather, I make an offer of proof that Ms. Hutchinson will testify that she was paying very careful attention to this location on the date in question because of having seen a jaywalker there just a week earlier.

13. The Court: Under Rule 403 I grant the request to strike the answer. It has some probative value, but I think the jury might use it for the inadmissible purpose of inferring that because O'Hare jaywalked on an earlier occasion, he did so on the date he was hit.

Def. Att: Would Your Honor consider "sanitizing" the evidence? In other words, allow my client to testify that she was driving especially carefully because she had seen a jaywalker at the same location a week earlier, but remove any reference to O'Hare in her testimony.

14. The Court: No, I'll deny that request as well. (In open court) Jurors, I have ruled that any evidence pertaining to an earlier incident, if any, involving Mr. O'Hare is inadmissible. I instruct you not to consider that testimony for any purpose.

Q: All right, Ms. Hutchinson, let's go back to the point when you're turning off Peach into Main. Did you notice anything unusual on the northeast corner of that intersection?

Pl. Att: Objection. The question is vague.

15. The Court: Overruled. The witness may answer.

A: Yes, as I was making the turn I saw 3 young children roughhousing a bit on the corner. It's a busy intersection, and I was afraid that someone would get hurt.

Pl. Att: Objection, Your Honor, irrelevant.

16. The Court: Overruled.

17. Q: Could you tell the approximate ages of the children?

18. A: I'd say about 8, 6 and 3.

19. Q: Ms. Hutchinson, were you issued a traffic ticket of any kind based on this incident?

　　 A: No.

(remainder of testimony omitted)

<u>Cross Examination by Plaintiff's Attorney</u>

　　 Q: Ms. Hutchinson, prior to striking Mr. O'Hare, had you consumed any alcoholic beverages that day?

　　 Def. Att: Objection, lack of foundation. There's no evidence that my client had had anything to drink.

　　 The Court: Any response?

　　 Pl. Att: I'm allowed to ask the question, Your Honor. The witness can tell us what the truth is.

20. The Court: I'll allow it. Witness may answer.

　　 A: Absolutely not.

　　 Q: Well, are you addicted to any narcotic drugs?

　　 Def. Att: Objection, objection! Lack of foundation.

　　 The Court: Counsel?

　　 Pl. Att: Same response, Your Honor. The witness can affirm or deny.

21. The Court: Well, I'll allow it, but then move on.

　　 Def. Att: I also object on the ground that

whether or not my client is at present addicted to narcotic drugs is irrelevant.

22. The Court: On that ground, the objection is sustained.

Q: Then I'll rephrase my question. At the time of this accident, September 22, were you addicted to any narcotic drugs?

Def. Att: Objection, irrelevant.

23. The Court: I'll still sustain the objection.

24. Q: Ms. Hutchinson, you are the sole owner of your contracting business, correct?

A: That's true.

25. Q: These children that you saw on the sidewalk, can you remember what they were wearing?

A: I'm sorry, I can't.

26. Q: Pretty selective memory you have, wouldn't you say?

A: I don't know what you mean.

Q: I'll move to something else. At the time you struck Mr. O'Hare, you were on your way to a construction project at 3rd and Main, correct?

Def. Att: Objection, asked and answered. I asked this question on direct.

27. The Court: Overruled. You may answer.

A: That's correct.

Q: And the reason you were going to that job is that an inspection had been missed, correct?

A: Yes.

Q: A missed inspection can delay work, right?

A: That's possible.

Q: You were upset, weren't you, that the inspection had been missed?

A: Not too much, it happens.

Q: But you were thinking about the missed inspection as you drove towards Main and 3rd, weren't you?

A: Maybe a little. But I am certain that your client was not in the crosswalk.

Pl. Att: Move to strike the last remark as nonresponsive, Your Honor.

28. The Court: What ruling?

29. Q: So your testimony is that even though you were annoyed by the missed inspection, you were concentrating on your driving?

A: That's correct.

Q: Mr. O'Hare appears to be of Hispanic descent, isn't that true?

A: That appears to be the case.

Q: And isn't it a fact that you've never hired a person of Hispanic descent to work for you?

Def. Att: Objection, Your Honor, irrelevant.

30. The Court: What ruling?

25

Transcript 5 (FRE 104, 401, 402, 403)

A. Background

See also, discussion preceding Transcript No. 4.

Physical objects offered into evidence are generally as subject to the rules of relevance as is oral testimony. However, physical objects may be admitted even though they lack independent evidentiary significance.

For example, assume that Jones testifies in a battery action against Smith that, "Smith hit me with a baseball bat." Jones then offers the baseball bat into evidence. The bat itself has no evidentiary significance independently of the testimony. However, such exhibits are often admitted on the basis that they illustrate and promote understanding of oral testimony.

Physical objects typically have greater impact on a judge or juror than oral testimony. The latter ends up as ink markings on a court stenographer's paper roll; the former often ends up in the jury room. Thus, judges tend to subject physical objects to close analysis pursuant to FRE 403. If an object offered into evidence varies in some significant way from the object described in a witness' oral testimony, or if an object is too complex to be readily understood, a judge may well exclude it.

To offer a physical object into evidence, a lawyer usually first marks it as an exhibit and shows it to opposing counsel, asks the witness to identify it, elicits whatever foundational information is necessary (e.g., that a letter is written in the hand of the party claimed to have written it), and asks that the judge receive it in evidence.

B. Testimony

State v. Pinsky

Ray Pinsky is charged with armed robbery, "taking the property of another through force or fear." The prosecution contends that Pinsky approached the victim, Joe Duffkin, with a knife as Duffkin was getting out of his car after arriving home from work. Pinsky allegedly demanded money, took Duffkin's wallet, and fled. Pinsky's defense is an alibi.

<u>Direct Examination of Joe Duffkin by Prosecutor</u>

Q: All right, Mr. Duffkin, what happened after you pulled into your driveway?

A: Just as I got out of my car, I heard someone behind me. I turned around, and that guy (pointing to Pinsky) was standing next to me with a knife.

Q: What effect did seeing the knife have on you?

1. A: I was really scared. I was afraid for my life.

Q: What happened next?

A: He told me to give him whatever money I had on me, and not to scream or try to get away.

Q: Did he say anything else?

2. A: Yeah, he said he had been doing armed robberies all his life, so I shouldn't try anything.

Q: Did you notice anything distinctive about the robber?

A: Yes, he spoke with a Southern accent.

Def. Att: Move to strike as irrelevant, Your Honor. Many people have a Southern accent; the evidence does not prove that my client was the robber.

3. The Court: What ruling?

Q: Had you ever seen the defendant previously?

4. A: Yes. Just a day or two earlier, as I was coming home from work, I noticed someone I hadn't seen before walking slowly a couple of blocks from my house. I'm pretty sure it was the defendant.

Q: Did you have an opportunity to observe the knife that the robber carried?

A: Yes, the blade was thin, and at least 7 or 8 inches long. It had a long brown handle.

Pros: Your Honor, I have a knife, which I've marked as State's Exhibit 1 and shown to defense counsel. May I approach the witness?

The Court: You may.

Q: Mr. Duffkin, showing you State's Exh. 1, do you recognize what it is?

A: Well, it's a knife of course. It's not exactly the same as the one he had--if anything, the blade of his knife was a little longer. But other than that, it's identical.

Pros: Your Honor, I offer Exh. 1 into evidence to help the jury understand the type of knife that the robber used.

The Court: You have not recovered the knife that was actually used?

Pros: No, Your Honor.

5. The Court: Exh. No. 1 will be received for illustrative purposes.

Q: Was it dark at the time of the robbery?

A: No, I'd guess you could say it was dusk.

6. Q: Did you have a good opportunity to observe the robber?

   A: Yes.

7. Q: Do you have any doubt that the defendant over here (pointing to Pinsky) is the person who robbed you?

   A: None whatsoever.

   Q: After he approached you with the knife, what happened?

   A: He told me to turn around, which I did. Then he reached into my pockets and took my wallet.

   Q: After your wallet was taken, what happened?

   A: He said that he would leave me a little reminder not to go to the cops, and he made a long slit down my back with his knife. Then he ran away.

   Q: He actually cut you?

   A: Yes.

   Pros: Your Honor, I'm holding a shirt which I've marked as State's Exh. 2 and shown to defense counsel. May I approach the witness?

   Def. Att: May we approach the bench? (At the bench) Your Honor, we object to the State offering this shirt into evidence. It is slit up the back and covered with dry blood. It is inflammatory, especially in view of the alibi defense.

   Pros: Your Honor, this is the actual shirt, and it demonstrates the violence of the robbery.

8. The Court: I'll keep it out. You may resume your places at counsel table. Any further questions?

Q: Just a few. After he ran away, did you find anything in the area where the robber was standing?

A: Yes, a small cellophane baggie. I took it inside and gave it to the police.

Pros: (At the bench) Your Honor, I intend to offer the baggie into evidence. I make an offer of proof that a police chemist will testify that the baggie contained remains of cocaine. We contend that the robber dropped it during the robbery, and that it suggests the motive for the robbery--the defendant was supporting a cocaine habit.

Def. Att: I object. The evidence is inflammatory.

9. The Court: What ruling?

Pros: Your Honor, I would also make an offer of proof that when the police arrested Pinsky in his apartment, they found a collection of paramilitary weaponry magazines all with subscription labels bearing his name and address. We intend to offer them as evidence of his interest in and ability to handle knives.

10. The Court: What response to the offer of proof?

Cross Examination by Defense Counsel

Q: Mr. Duffkin, what time did you arrive home on the day you were robbed?

A: At 5:30.

Q: You're sure of that?

A: Yes.

Q: Well, what time did you arrive home the day before the robbery?

Pros. Att: Objection, irrelevant.

11. The Court: Sustained.

   Q: Mr. Duffkin, you had a business lunch the day of the robbery, did you not?

   A: Yes, I did.

12. Q: And between 1 and 2:30, you consumed 3 martinis, correct?

   A: Well, that was with lunch.

13. Q: When did you decide to accuse Mr. Pinsky of the robbery?

   A: What do you mean?

   Q: Well, the thing that scared you most was the knife, correct?

   A: That's true.

   Q: When you first turned around, your attention was on that knife?

   A: A lot.

   Q: Then the robber ordered you to turn around so that you were facing away from him?

   A: Yes.

   Q: Mr. Duffkin, I'm going to ask you to step down and stand over here. I'll ask that the courtroom lights be turned off; there will still be some light in here. An individual is going to stand next to you. I'm going to ask you to turn around, look at that individual momentarily, then turn away from him. Then I'm going to ask 5 people, including that individual, to come into the courtroom and ask you to pick out the one you saw.

14. Pros: You are the Prosecutor. What objections, if any, would you make?

Chapter 3

Hearsay

Transcript 6 (FRE 801)

A. Background

Assertions made other than by a witness when testifying are inadmissible hearsay if they are offered for the truth of the matter asserted. Developed hundreds of years ago in England for the purpose of tormenting future generations of lawyers, the rule distinguishes between hearsay (statements offered for their truth) and non-hearsay (statements offered for a purpose other than their truth).

Every assertion has a myriad of potential "not for the truth of the matter asserted" uses. For example, the statement, "The Dodgers beat the Giants, 8-4," can be offered to prove that (a) the speaker was alive at the moment the words were spoken; (b) the speaker is familiar with the game of baseball; (c) the speaker believed that the Dodgers had beaten the Giants; (d) the person to whom the words were spoken, a Giants' fan, was disconsolate; etc. When an out-of-court statement is offered for a purpose other than its truth, the frequent issue becomes the relevance of the non-hearsay use.

If a person engages in conduct as a substitute for making a verbal assertion, the conduct is hearsay if the assertion would have been. For example, assume that following an accident, an officer asks a bystander, "How fast was the blue car going?" Rather than answering, the bystander (a Harpo Marx wanna-be?) jumps in his car and drives past the officer at 60 m.p.h. Offered to prove that the blue car was being driven 60 m.p.h., the act of driving will probably be regarded as the equivalent of the statement, "He was going 60 m.p.h.," and thus hearsay.

Assertions may also be implied from statements that are non-assertive in form.

Assume that a person answers a knock at the front door, and says, "Hi, Joan." Offered to prove that Joan was at the front door, the words are likely to be deemed to imply the assertion, "Joan is here," and thus to constitute hearsay.

B. <u>Testimony</u>

<u>Estate of J. Paul Giddy</u>

Will contest action brought by the decedent's daughter, Vera, in an effort to set aside her late father's will as the product of insane delusions. The will, dated June 28 of the year before Giddy's death, leaves Giddy's entire estate to a charity, Save the Easter Seals. Testifying on Vera's behalf is Howard Huge, formerly a close personal friend of the decedent.

<u>Direct Examination by Counsel for Contestant</u>

(Preliminary questioning omitted)

    Q: Mr. Huge, do you recall the evening of July 2 of the year before Mr. Giddy's death?

    A: I do. I was at Mr. Giddy's house for dinner.

1. Q: How is it you can be certain that you were together that particular evening?

2. A: I remember because it was the same day that my stockbroker had told me to be sure to buy shares in a company called Hugh's Tool Co., because they were part of a new issue that she thought would skyrocket.

    Q: Please tell us what you had for dinner that night.

    Respondent's Att: Objection, Your Honor, irrelevant.

    Contestant's Att: Your Honor, this is

offered to show the clarity of the witness' recollection of the details of that particular evening.

3. The Court: I'll sustain the objection.

Q: All right, let's move on, Mr. Huge. Do you recall a conversation you and Mr. Giddy had after dinner?

A: I do.

Q: Please tell us what if anything Mr. Giddy said about his family during this conversation.

A: He said that Vera was just waiting for him to die so that she could inherit his money and pay off gambling debts.

Respondent's Att: Objection and move to strike as hearsay. Also, anything said by Mr. Giddy after the will was executed is irrelevant.

4. The Court: Overruled.

Q: Did you ever tell anyone else that Giddy had made this statement to you?

5. A: Yes, when I got home that evening I told my wife what Giddy had told me.

Q: Had Mr. Giddy ever made a similar statement to you?

A: Yes, it was about 2 years earlier. We were taking a walk, and he said something about Vera owing millions to the Mafia.

Respondent's Att: Same hearsay and relevance objections.

6. The Court: Same rulings.

7. Q: Was Mr. Giddy just kidding around?

A: No, I'm sure he meant it.

Q: Had you ever heard of Mr. Giddy making remarks about his family members to other people?

A: Yes. The next day, another friend of Giddy's and mine, Rocky Feller, told me that Giddy had recently told him, "Everyone in my family is deeply in debt to the Mafia because they do nothing but gamble and drink."

Respondent's Att: Objection to Feller's statement, hearsay.

8. The Court: Sustained.

Q: Without using Feller's exact words, can you give us the gist of what Feller told you that Giddy said?

A: Giddy basically told Feller the same thing about gambling that Giddy had told me the night before.

Respondent's Att: Objection, hearsay.

9. The Court: Sustained.

Q: Let me ask it this way. Without telling us anything that Mr. Feller told you, was it your belief after talking to him that Mr. Giddy had made the same remark about gambling to Mr. Feller that he had made to you?

10. Respondent's Att: What if any objection would you make?

Q: Mr. Huge, let me turn your attention to the afternoon of June 13, about a week before Mr. Giddy executed his will. Do you recall that date?

A: I do.

Q: Did you see Mr. Giddy on that date?

A: I stopped by his apartment, but didn't actually see him.

Q: What happened?

A: Well, I had knocked on the front door of his apartment, but gotten no answer. Then I heard a couple of voices coming from down the hallway. I heard someone ask, "How are the kids?"

Q: Do you know whose voice this was?

A: No, I didn't recognize it at all.

Q: All right, please continue.

A: I heard a different person say, "My poor daughter is dead." Then the first person said, "No she's not, she called you last week, remember?" Then the second voice said, "I'm crazy as a nuthouse."

Q: Did you recognize this second voice?

A: Being down the corridor and everything, it was hard to tell, but I'd say the second voice was Giddy's.

Q: Did you try to see who it was?

A: Yes, I turned the corner and walked down the corridor, but couldn't see anyone. So I just went home.

Q: What leads you to say the second voice was that of Mr. Giddy?

A: I've known him for years, it just sounded like him.

Respondent's Att: Objection to this conversation, on the ground that the witness lacks sufficient personal knowledge as to whether the second voice was that of the decedent.

11. The Court: The question is whether the jury could reasonably conclude that the voice was that of Mr. Giddy.

12. **The Court:** Let me ask some additional questions by way of foundation. On the average, how often had you spoken to Mr. Giddy in the year prior to this hallway conversation?

    A: That's hard to say. Sometimes I'd talk to him 2 or 3 times a week, other times not for a few weeks.

    The Court: And had you ever correctly identified his voice by hearing it when you couldn't see Mr. Giddy?

    A: No.

13. **The Court:** The issue is close, but I find the foundation sufficient to allow the jury to conclude that the second voice was that of Mr. Giddy.

    Respondent's Att: Also object to what the second person said as hearsay.

14. **The Court:** Overruled.

Cross Examination by Respondent's Counsel

    Q: Mr. Huge, do you know Ivana Frump?

    A: Yes, she's a neighbor of mine.

15. **Q:** Didn't you tell her just a week ago, "I feel awful that Giddy cut off Vera without a cent. She deserves to get a lot of his money."

    A: I may have.

    Q: Isn't it a fact that you did make that statement?

    Pl. Att: Objection, argumentative.

16. **The Court:** Overruled.

    A: I probably did say that.

Q: Now, you testified to a statement about goldfish that Mr. Giddy made on June 26, correct?

A: I did.

17. Q: Didn't Mr. Giddy also tell you during that conversation that Vera had no respect for the value of money, and that she was a big disappointment to him?

18. A: That's true. But I told him that he was wrong, that in fact Vera was very careful with money.

Transcript 7 (FRE 801)

   A. <u>Background</u>

   See discussion accompanying Transcript 6.

   B. <u>Testimony</u>

   <u>Keaton v. Brooks</u>

   Civil action for assault and battery brought by plaintiff Mia Keaton against defendant Woody Brooks. Keaton claims that Brooks struck her numerous times with a windshield cleaning tool at a "Jet" self-service gas station. Brooks denies striking Keaton, and in the alternative contends that any action he may have taken with regard to Keaton was in self defense. Testifying on plaintiff Keaton's behalf is Ann Hall, who was present at the gas station at the time of the incident.

<u>Direct Examination by Plaintiff's Counsel</u>

   Q: Please state your name.

   Def. Att: Objection, hearsay.

1. The Court: Overruled, you may answer.

   A: Ann Hall.

   Q: Were you at the Jet gas station on Melish Rd. on the afternoon of February 14?

   A: I was.

   Q: What time was this?

2. A: It was exactly 4 o'clock. I know because just as I pulled in I heard the radio announcer say, "Time for the 4 o'clock news."

   Q: And what if anything occurred at that time?

3. A: I had been waiting in line for a few minutes, and when it was my turn and I

got out of my car to pump gas, I someone yell, "This is ridiculous. I've never had to wait this long for gas in my life."

4. Q: You later found out that the person who said this was defendant Brooks?

   A: That's right.

   Q: What tone of voice was this said in?

5. A: He sounded very angry, like a wild beast.

   Q: How did you react?

6. A: I was frightened. I told the friend who was riding with me that the guy could be dangerous, because I had looked over and seen that he was holding a windshield washer tool.

   Q: Then what happened?

7. A: He walked over to her (pointing to plaintiff) and told her to stop pumping gas or he'd beat the stuffing out of her.

   Q: Can you remember his exact words?

   Def. Att: Objection, asked and answered.

8. The Court: Sustained

   Q: Did Ms. Keaton reply?

9. A: Yes, she told him to stay away from her, that she was a black belt in karate.

10. Q: Why did she say this?

    A: She was clearly scared, and wanted to frighten him off.

    Q: Then what happened?

A: I started pumping gas, hoping to get out of there fast.

Q: Did you see Ms. Keaton and the defendant again?

11. A: Yes, I looked up when I heard someone at the next pump say, "He's hitting her over the head for no reason." Ms. Keaton was bent over, and the defendant was hitting her in the back of the head.

Q: How many times did you see the defendant strike Ms. Keaton?

A: I don't recall exactly.

Q: Might it refresh your recollection if you looked at your deposition?

A: That's possible.
(Counsel identifies page and line of deposition, shows it to the witness, and takes it back.)

Q: Now, how many times did you see him strike Ms. Keaton?

12. A: According to my deposition, it was 5 times.

13. Q: Did you also testify in the deposition that after he stopped hitting Ms. Keaton, the defendant said, "Serves you right."?

A: Yes.

Q: Then what happened?

A: The defendant threw down the windshield washer tool, ran to his car and drove off.

Q: Did you notice anything about his car?

14. A: Yes, it had a strange personalized license plate which read, "Lik 2 Fite."

15. Q: One last question. Are you personally acquainted with either of the parties to this action?

   A: No I am not.

Cross Examination by Defense Counsel

   Q: Ms. Hall, isn't it true that you have a medical condition that has caused you to lose 50% of your hearing ability?

   Pl. Att: Objection, beyond the scope of direct. I asked her nothing about her physical condition.

16. The Court: What ruling?

   Pl. Att: Also object as hearsay; counsel is trying to elicit a hearsay statement of her doctor.

17. The Court: What ruling?

   Q: Let's move on. A few weeks after this incident, my client called you at your place of business, correct?

   A: Yes.

18. Q: And he was polite and courteous at that time, right?

   A: Yes.

19. Q: And he told you that he thought Ms. Keaton was going to attack him with a knife?

   A: That's what he said.

20. Q: And you said, did you not, that everything happened so fast, you couldn't tell what had happened?

   A: I did, but the reason is that...

   Q: Thank you, you've answered my question. Now...

Pl. Att: Your Honor, I ask that the witness be allowed to explain why she might have made that statement.

21. The Court: Denied. You can elicit the explanation during redirect if you choose to do so.

Transcript 8 (FRE 801)

A. Background

See discussion accompanying Transcript 6.

B. Testimony

State v. Dunne

Criminal prosecution of Cedric Dunne for the murder of his former fiance, Dominique Nichols. The prosecution contends that Dunne struck Nichols with his fists so severely that she died. In addition, the prosecution intends to prove that the fatal beating was one of many that Dunne had administered to Nichols over their months of cohabiting. The defendant admits striking Nichols on the night that she died, but claims that her death accidentally resulted from a fall after she was struck. Moreover, he claims that he struck her in self-defense, after she threatened him and advanced on him with a kitchen knife.

Called as a witness for the prosecution is Yolanda Sweeney. She has testified to her personal background, and to her close friendship with the decedent.

Direct Examination by Prosecuting Attorney

Q: Ms. Sweeney, when was the next time that you saw Dominique?

A: A couple of days later, on the 23rd, I think.

Q: That was just 2 days before her death?

A: Yes.

Q: At that time, did she talk to you about her relationship with Mr. Dunne?

A: Yes, she did.

Q: What did she tell you?

A: For one thing, she said that Dunne was always getting mad at her and hitting her.

Def. Att: Objection, Your Honor, hearsay.

Pros: Your Honor, the statement is non-hearsay, because it's not offered for it's truth. We can infer from the statement that Ms. Nichols was afraid of the defendant, and from that fear infer that it is unlikely that she would attack him.

1. The Court: I'll admit the statement as non-hearsay.

Def. Att: I also object under FRE 403 that the minimal relevance of the statement for non-truth purposes is outweighed by the prejudice to Mr. Dunne. The jury is likely to use it as evidence that he did in fact hit Ms. Nichols repeatedly even though Your Honor has admitted it for a limited purpose.

2. The Court: Counsel, once a legitimate non-hearsay use has been identified, the evidence is admissible. Let's proceed with the testimony, counsel.

Q: Did she say anything else?

3. A: Since we're appearing in a transcript that emphasizes hearsay problems, you know very well that she did. She also told me that she had heard that Dunne once killed a person.

Q: Was this the first time you had heard such things about Mr. Dunne?

4. A: Oh, no. A few days before, a friend of mine and Dominique's also told me that Dunne had been hitting Dominique.

Q: Now, during this conversation with Dominique on the 23rd, did she say anything about what she was planning to do?

5. A: Yes. She said that as soon as she could she was going to tell Dunne to move out of her apartment.

Q: Did you observe anything unusual about Dominique's physical condition when you spoke with her on the 23rd?

A: Yes, I noticed some large red welts on her right arm.

Q: And what if anything took place with respect to those welts?

6. A: Well, I asked if Dunne had done that to her. She immediately broke down and started crying.

Q: I'd now like to turn your attention to the evening of Ms. Nichols' death. Where were you at about 6:30 that evening?

A: I was going to Dominique's apartment. I wanted to see if Dunne had moved out.

Q: And what happened when you arrived there?

A: From outside the door, I could hear Dunne's voice; he was speaking very loudly.

Q: What did you hear him say?

7. A: He said, "I've had it with you, I'm not going to take it anymore."

Q: What next happened?

A: A Mr. Tobias, who lives next door, opened the door of his apartment and told me that he had never heard anyone carry on for so long in such an angry voice.

Def. Att: Objection and move to strike, hearsay.

Pros: Your Honor, we're not trying to prove the statement's literal truth, but only as a basis for inferring that the defendant was extremely angry. Therefore it's not hearsay.

8. The Court: What ruling?

   Q: Did you reply?

9. A: Yes, I said that he sounded angry enough to kill someone.

   Q: What if anything did you do?

   A: I ran into Tobias's apartment to call the police.

   Def. Att: Objection, hearsay. The testimony is the equivalent of the witness' out of court statement that Mr. Dunne was behaving violently.

10. The Court: Objection overruled.

    Q: Then what happened? (remainder of testimony omitted)

Cross Examination by Defense Counsel

   Q: Ms. Sweeney, you talked to Mr. Dunne about 3 weeks after Ms. Nichols' death, when he was in jail, didn't you?

   A: Yes.

11. Q: And at that time he told you that he had acted in self-defense, didn't he?

    A: I do recall that.

    Q: About 3 weeks ago, you also spoke with Vivian Ihori, an investigator from my office, correct?

    A: Yes.

    Q: And didn't you tell Ms. Ihori that when you went to Ms. Nichols' apartment on the day she died, you didn't see Mr. Tobias until after the police arrived?

Pros: Objection, Your Honor, as the prior statement was not under oath, it is improper impeachment.

12. The Court: Sustained.

13. Q: Let me ask you about something else, Ms. Sweeney. Isn't it a fact that you told Ms. Ihori that Ms. Nichols once told you, "I've got to get Sweeney before he gets me?"

    A: I think I did say that to her.

14. Q: You testified that when you spoke with Ms. Nichols on the 23rd, you noticed a couple of red spots on her right arm. Do you recall whether she was bandaged in any way?

    A: I don't remember.

15. Q: According to Ms. Ihori, Ms. Nichols was not bandaged in any way. Is Ms. Ihori incorrect about that?

    A: I'm just saying I don't remember anything about bandages.

    Q: Ms. Sweeney, you know a Derek Kent, correct?

    A: Yes, he's a good friend.

16. Q: Isn't it true that you told him about a month before Ms. Nichols' death that you thought Mr. Dunne was a big jerk who you wanted to see get his comeuppance?

    A: I probably did say that.

(Remainder of examination omitted)

The second witness called by the prosecutor is Officer Matt Leslie. Leslie has already testified to his background and his role in the investigation of Ms. Nichols' death.

<u>Direct Examination by Prosecuting Attorney</u>

- Q: Off. Leslie, when you arrived at Ms. Nichols' apartment, what happened?

- A: I knocked on the door and identified myself as a police officer. The door was opened by the individual seated there (indicating the defendant, Dunne). I entered, accompanied by a Ms. Sweeney, briefly examined Ms. Nichols, and called an ambulance.

- Q: For probable cause-- what then happened?

17. A: I asked Ms. Sweeney if she could identify the male individual whose voice she had heard from outside the door. She pointed to Mr. Dunne.

- Q: Then what happened?

18. A: She began crying, hit Mr. Dunne on the chest and repeated something like, "Why'd you do it?" a few times. Dunne said nothing.

- Q: Then what happened?

- A: While I was placing Mr. Dunne under arrest, a man identifying himself as Robert Tobias came in. He gave me a piece of paper on which he said he had written exactly what he had heard Mr. Dunne saying.

- Q: Officer, I show you State's # 3 for identification, a piece of paper signed by Robert Tobias. Please examine it and tell us if this is the sheet of paper he handed to you.

- A: Yes it is.

- Pros: Your Honor, I ask that Exh. # 3 be received in evidence.

19. The Court: What ruling?

    Q: You testified that you placed Mr. Dunne under arrest. Before doing so, did you speak with him?

    A: Yes, I asked him what had happened. He told me...

    Def. Att: Objection. As this appears to have been a custodial interrogation, there's no foundation for any statements made by Mr. Dunne to the police officer.

20. The Court: Before the officer can testify to any statement made by Mr. Dunne to the police officer, the prosecution has the burden of proving by a preponderance of the evidence either that this was not a custodial interrogation, or that the interrogation complied with the strictures of <u>Miranda</u>.

21. The Court: To save time, I'll permit the jurors to remain during the foundational testimony, and instruct them to disregard the testimony if I conclude that the defendant's statements to the officer are inadmissible. Prosecutor may inquire.

<u>Voir Dire Examination of Off. Leslie by Prosecutor</u>

    Q: Officer Leslie, what happened after you called the ambulance?

    A: I patted Mr. Dunne down for weapons; he was unarmed.

    Q: Please continue.

22. A: At that point he said he wanted to make a statement.

    Q: What were you doing at this time?

A: I was trying to do what I could to help Ms. Nichols. I was administering CPR, and working with Ms. Sweeney to try to stop Ms. Nichols from bleeding to death.

Q: Did you nevertheless reply to Mr. Dunne?

23. A: I just told him to stop bothering us, that he could leave if he wanted to.

24. Q: In your opinion, did Mr. Dunne understand that he was not in custody at that time?

A: I am confident that he did.

Q: What did he say?

A: He said that he really needed to say something.

Q: And when he spoke to you, what were you doing?

A: I was still in the process of administering CPR to Ms. Nichols.

Pros: Your Honor, at this time I ask that this audiocassette, which I have previously played for defense counsel, be marked People's # 1 for identification.

The Court: Counsel, please make an offer of proof as to the contents of Exh. # 1. Both counsel please approach the bench for this purpose.

Pros: (At the bench) The audiocassette is a recording of the conversation between Officer Leslie and Mr. Dunne in Ms. Nichols' apartment. The officer has a small recording unit that he activates when talking to potential suspects; he did so on this occasion.

The Court: Defense counsel, any objections?

Def. Att: Object as hearsay; the tape is the speakers' out-of-court statements.

25. The Court: That objection is overruled.

    Def. Att: Also object that the tape is cumulative. The officer has already testified as to the conversation.

26. The Court: I'll sustain that objection. (remainder of direct examination omitted)

    The Court: Defense Counsel, any questions on voir dire?

    Def. Att: None, Your Honor. Submitted.

27. The Court: Based on the foundational showing, I find that there was not a custodial interrogation, and I'll permit the officer to testify as to the defendant's statements.

Chapter 4

Hearsay Exceptions Not Requiring Unavailability

Transcript 9: "Admissions and Business Records"
(FRE 801, 803)

A. <u>Background</u>

Hearsay statements which do not qualify for admission into evidence occupy increasingly less shelf space in the evidence rules supermarket. Intruding into hearsay's place are statutorily-defined exceptions which do not require the declarant to be unavailable, statutorily-defined exceptions which do require unavailability, the catch-all or "wild card" hearsay exceptions, and hearsay exemptions. Added to these, of course, is non-hearsay use of statements. No wonder experts debate whether the hearsay rule or the manatee shall first cease to exist.

The Federal Rules classify perhaps the most commonly-used hearsay exception, "admissions," as a hearsay <u>exemption</u>. (FRE 801) The change in terminology has not affected the underlying rule that statements made by a party are admissible when offered <u>against</u> the party who made them. Statements qualify as party admissions even if they are not inculpatory, and even if they are not made under circumstances suggesting reliability. What this means is that everything you have ever said is a potential admissible admission, merely awaiting the coming of your being a party to a lawsuit which makes your statement relevant.

Reliability is, by contrast, the factor that unites most of the exceptions which do not require that the declarant be unavailable. A "present sense impression" (FRE 803(1)) is at least arguably reliable because memory lapses are unlikely. The startling events that produce "excited utterances" (FRE 803(2)) are often memorable, and such events may override any conscious desire to fabricate.

Other common hearsay exceptions rest on a combination of reliability and necessity. "Declarations of present state of mind" (FRE 803(3)) may often be reliable: memory problems are few when people assert their then-existing beliefs and emotions. But in addition, they are often necessary. Substantive outcomes often depend on the state of mind with which an act was done; lacing Aunt Lucy's tea with arsenic may be an unfortunate accident, negligence or murder, depending largely on the lacer's mental state. With so much riding on mental factors, the need arises to admit assertions of state of mind.

The same combination of reliability and necessity is behind the admissibility of "business records" (FRE 803(6)). As most businesses rely upon accurate records in their daily operations, and as business records tend to be produced regularly and repeatedly, the records are likely to be trustworthy. In addition, typical business records pass through many employee's hands. It would be burdensome and in some cases impossible to trace their path in court. An employee who can identify a record and testify to its reliable mode of preparation is generally all that a court requires.

B. <u>Testimony</u>

<u>Palmer v. Dunbar</u>

Plaintiff Susan Palmer contends that defendant Brad Dunbar discriminated against her on the basis of her gender by firing her from her employment as an employee of a bookstore owned by Dunbar. Dunbar admits firing Palmer, but contends that it was for reasons of poor work performance (reporting to work late and alienating customers by complaining about the "trashy" materials the book store had begun carrying after Dunbar's purchase of the bookstore) and had nothing to do with Palmer's gender.

Evidence thus far introduced establishes that Dunbar bought the bookstore from its former owner, Justin Tyme, about 6 months before firing Palmer. At the time Dunbar bought the shop, it was managed by Martha Olsen. Olsen quit, however, about 2 months after the shop was sold. Below is a partial transcript of Olsen's testimony; she was called as a witness by Palmer.

Direct Examination of Martha Olsen by Counsel for Plaintiff

(The witness has thus far testified that she had been manager of the bookshop for about 12 years when Dunbar bought it, that Palmer had been employed there for 10 years, and that during most of this time the bookshop employed 6-7 salespeople.)

    Q: Ms. Olsen, your testimony is that you were Ms. Palmer's supervisor during the period that both you and she were employed at the bookshop?

    A: That's correct, yes.

1. Q: And prior to Mr. Dunbar purchasing the book store, how was her work performance as compared to that of the other employees?

    A: She was among the best. She kept up with many fields and often was able to help customers select books.

    Q: Did Mr. Tyme ever say anything about Ms. Palmer's work performance?

2. A: Yes, on a number of occasions he said he thought that she was our most valuable employee.

    Q: Now, when Mr. Dunbar took over as the new owner on January 1, was he regularly in the store?

    A: No, he'd come in about once a week. He was mostly involved with some other businesses.

3. Q: Do you remember a conversation about Ms. Palmer that Mr. Dunbar had with

Q: you on January 5, shortly after he bought the shop?

A: I do.

Q: And what did Mr. Dunbar tell you about Ms. Palmer?

4. A: He said that Susan Palmer was a very attractive employee. He asked me if Ms. Palmer was married, and when I said that I thought she was divorced he said that he was going to try to find out more about her.

Q: How did you respond?

5. A: I said that the bookstore was always a place where we respected employees' privacy, that I felt that Ms. Palmer was very sensitive, and that I intended to do whatever I could to protect her privacy and her feelings.

Q: Shortly thereafter, did you have a conversation with Ms. Palmer?

A: Yes, I'd say a day or two later.

Q: And what did she tell you?

6. A: She said she was very upset, because Mr. Dunbar had asked her to have a drink after work.

Q: Did she say anything else?

7. A: Yes. She said she was going to meet with Mr. Dunbar in the bookstore the next day, and tell him that she wanted nothing to do with him socially.

Q: What's the next thing that happened?

8. A: A few minutes later, I saw Ms. Palmer using the phone at the rear of the shop. She seemed to be on hold, so I asked her who she was talking to. She said she was talking to Mr. Dunbar, and that she was telling him

		that she wanted to have nothing to do with him.
	Q:	How did that affect you?
9.	A:	I was glad she was telling him to stop his abusive conduct.
	Q:	Ms. Olsen, I'd like to call your attention to an episode in late January. Do you recall a customer making a statement to you about Ms. Palmer?
	A:	I do, but not too well to tell you the truth.
	Q:	Well, did you make a note of the comment?
10.	A:	I think I did, because I thought that Mr. Dunbar was probably going to cause problems in the future for Ms. Palmer.
	Q:	Ms. Olsen, I hand you plaintiff's Exh. 3, which I have shown to counsel for Mr. Dunbar. Please look over Exh. 3, and tell us what it is.
	A:	This is a note I made about what a customer told me about Susan Palmer. I put it in her personnel folder.
11.	Q:	You recognize your handwriting?
	A:	Yes, it's my handwriting.
	Q:	Do you recall when you made this note?
	A:	As best I can remember, the same day the customer made the remark to me, probably after work. No later than the next day, for sure.
	Q:	Was the customer's statement fresh in your mind when you wrote out this note?
	Def. Att:	Objection, Your Honor. Calls for a legal conclusion.

12. The Court: I agree. Counsel, rephrase the question.

    Q: At the time you wrote the note, were you able to remember clearly what the customer told you?

    Def. Att: Same objection, Your Honor.

13. The Court: No, I'll overrule the objection. The witness may answer.

    A: Yes, I was.

    Q: And what did you write down?

    A: Just what the customer told me.

    Q: Ms. Olsen, could you please read what is written on Exh. 3?

    A: All right. It says, "January 23. A man named Sidney Winter told me that Susan Palmer had been extremely helpful to him. He said he had needed a book of off-color jokes for a fraternity party, and that Susan Palmer had found just the right one. He said she was very friendly and helpful." Then there's my signature, "Martha Olsen."

    Def. Att: Objection, Your Honor. Inadmissible hearsay of Ms. Olsen.

14. The Court: I should admit the evidence as long as there is sufficient evidence from which the jury could reasonably conclude that the statement was made in the regular course of business.

15. The Court: Overruled; the statement qualifies as the witness' recorded recollection.

16. The Court: I'd also admit it as a business record.

    Def. Att: Also object that the testimony

constitutes inadmissible hearsay of Sidney Winter.

17. The Court: I'll overrule that objection.

   Q: Plaintiff asks that Exh. 3 be received in evidence, Your Honor.

18. The Court: What ruling?

   Q: Ms. Olsen, as manager of the bookstore, was it your duty to maintain the personnel files of all employees?

   A: Yes.

   Q: And if customers made remarks to you about any employee, positive or negative, would you try to make a note of it in that employee's personnel file?

   A: Yes, I'd usually just jot a note on a piece of paper and put it in the file.

   Q: Were other employees asked to do likewise?

   A: Yes.

   Q: Have you reviewed Ms. Palmer's personnel file for the period during which you were the store manager after Mr. Dunbar purchased the bookstore?

   A: I have.

19. Q: And according to Ms. Palmer's personnel file, did customers make any negative reports about Ms. Palmer during that period of time?

   A: No, they did not.

20. Q: Ms. Olsen, I'd like to turn your attention to another matter. Do you recall a meeting in early February with Susan Palmer in the storeroom

> in the back of the bookstore when Ms. Palmer was in tears?

A: Yes, very well.

Q: Can you remember when in early February this conversation took place?

A: Probably around the 5th or 6th, sorry I can't be any more specific. It was in the late afternoon, I do remember.

Q: Could you please describe what happened?

Def. Att: Objection, calls for a narrative response.

21. The Court: Overruled, witness may answer.

Q: Well, I remember I was discussing ordering a book for a customer with another employee. Ms. Palmer grabbed my arm and said she had to talk to me right then. I could see her eyes were red and she was shaking, so I walked her back to the storeroom where we could talk in private. She immediately burst into tears and said she didn't know what to do. She said that Mr. Dunbar had told her that he wanted her to attend an out-of-town book convention with him, and that it would be his chance to get to know her a lot better. She also said that for the past few weeks he'd been asking her out to drinks and for dinner meetings, and she didn't know how much longer she could handle it.

Def. Att: Objection to what Palmer told her, hearsay.

22. The Court: Overruled, it is non-hearsay as it indicated to the witness why Ms. Palmer was upset.

23. The Court: Even if the statement is admitted for its truth, it qualifies as an excited utterance.

Q: Did you ever discuss this conversation with Mr. Dunbar?

A: I did say something to him a day or so later when he came to the store to discuss some new materials he wanted to stock.

Q: What did you say to him?

A: I asked whether he was going to attend the upcoming book convention.

Q: And how did Mr. Dunbar respond?

A: He said that he was going to attend, and that he hoped Ms. Palmer would go with him to learn the business. At the same time he mentioned Ms. Palmer learning the business, he winked at me.

Def. Att: Objection and move to strike the wink testimony, conclusion.

24. The Court: Overruled.

Q: What did Mr. Dunbar mean by the wink?

Def. Att: Objection, improper opinion.

25. The Court: What ruling?

26. Q: One final question before the recess, Ms. Olsen. Based on everything that went on, were you surprised to learn that Ms. Palmer had filed a sexual harassment suit?

A: Not at all.

The Court: We'll take the luncheon recess at this time.

Transcript 10: "Vicarious Admissions" (FRE 801, 803)

A. Background

In their purest form, admissions consist of the introduction into evidence of parties' own statements. "Impure" admissions also exist, in a manner of speaking-- or rather, in a manner of not speaking. Under FRE 801, parties may be held accountable for statements made by someone else. For example, if a party fails to respond to an assertion in a situation in which a judge believes that a reasonable person would have responded, the judge may admit the assertion as though it were the party's. Similarly, an assertion by a party's employee concerning a matter within the scope of employment qualifies as the party's admission.

The admissions doctrine typically rides roughshod over other potential obstacles to admissibility. For instance, evidence rules forbid witnesses from testifying without personal knowledge or to conclusions of law. Often, hearsay assertions which might satisfy one hearsay exception or another but which are similarly tainted are barred to the same extent in-court testimony would be forbidden. But if an assertion qualifies as an admission, personal or vicarious, such shortcomings matter little. A trial is war, and war is hell! If a party makes an assertion, or the law imputes an assertion to the party, into evidence it comes. It is then up to the party to rebut the assertion before the trier by explaining, e.g., "Maybe I said that, but that was in haste, before I knew what really happened."

B. Testimony

Palmer v. Dunbar
(Same Case as Transcript 9)

Continued Direct of Martha Olsen by Counsel for Palmer

1. Q: Ms. Olsen, before the lunch recess you had testified that you maintained

employee personnel files, is that correct?

A: Yes, that's correct.

2. Q: Would those files include records of the number of times that employees either failed to arrive or were late arriving for work?

A: Yes.

Q: Could you briefly describe how these records were maintained?

A: It was pretty straightforward. Mr. Dunbar installed a time clock, and each employee would punch in upon arrival. At the end of each week, my assistant, George Harrison, would review each employee's time card. If an employee was more than 15 minutes late, Mr. Harrison would note the date the employee was tardy, the time the employee was supposed to have reported, and the time the employee actually arrived on a separate "Tardy" sheet in each employee's personnel file. Unless Harrison reported to me that a particular employee was repeatedly late, I would not look at the Tardy sheets until an employee's formal evaluation was conducted, each 6 months.

3. Q: Your Honor, I ask that this Sheet of paper, entitled "Tardy sheet" and demonstrating that the claim that Palmer was fired for reporting late to work was just a pretext of the defendant, be marked Plaintiff's No. 7 for identification. I am showing it to defense counsel.

The Court: It may be so marked.

Q: Ms. Olsen, I hand you Exhibit 7 and ask if you recognize it.

A: Yes, this is the Tardy sheet from Susan Palmer's personnel file beginning from the time Mr. Dunbar bought the bookstore.

Q: How do you recognize it?

A: Well, it's the form we used, it's got Ms. Palmer's name on it, and this looks like Harrison's handwriting.

Q: Your Honor, I ask that Exhibit 7 be received in evidence.

4. The Court: I should admit the document if the plaintiff shows by a preponderance of the evidence that the foundation required by FRE 803 (6) has been shown.

5. The Court: Plaintiff's 7 will be received in evidence.

Q: Ms. Olsen, according to Plaintiff's 7, how often was Susan Palmer more than 15 minutes late to work in the two months following Mr. Dunbar's purchase of the bookstore?

Def. Att: Objection. The document speaks for itself.

6. The Court: I'll let the witness answer.

A: Three times, once in January and twice in February.

Q: Compared to other employees of the bookshop, was there anything unusual about that number of tardies?

Def. Att: Objection, vague.

7. The Court: Overruled.

A: Not really, pretty typical I'd say, though she was tardy during those months more often than she was before Mr. Dunbar bought the shop.

Q: Do you know why her tardiness increased after Mr. Dunbar bought the bookshop?

8. A: I remember that one day that she was late she told me that she was afraid that Mr. Dunbar was going to make sexual advances towards her, so she came in a little late in the hope that he would have left.

Def. Att: If the prior answer is to be allowed, I ask that the jury be admonished not to consider the statement as evidence that Mr. Dunbar made sexual advances towards the plaintiff.

9. The Court: What response to defense counsel's request?

Q: Do you recall a meeting you had with Mr. Dunbar concerning Ms. Palmer in late February?

A: I do.

Q: How did this meeting come about?

A: He said that he was very concerned about Palmer's suitability as an employee, and he wanted to talk to me about letting her go. We met the next day.

Q: Please tell us what happened at the meeting.

10. A: It was very short. What I remember is that he told me that he wanted me to fire Palmer for poor work performance. I said, "Isn't the real reason her refusal of your sexual advances?" He just said, "You've got your instructions," and he walked out.

Q: How did you respond to this?

A: I was very upset. I immediately wrote a note to Mr. Dunbar saying that I thought he was sexually harassing Susan Palmer, and asking him not to fire her and to stop harassing her. I left the note on his desk the same night. He never responded to it.

11. Def. Att: Objection, lack of foundation. There's no evidence that Dunbar ever saw the note.

12. Def. Att: Object further that testimony about the contents of the note violates the Original Writing Rule.

13. Def. Att: Object further that the witness' written note is a hearsay statement to which Mr. Dunbar was not required to respond.

The Court: (Rulings omitted.)

Q: Now, Ms. Olsen, did you meet with Susan Palmer following your late February meeting with Mr. Dunbar?

A: I did. I told her that I had to let her go. Susan became angry and upset, and said, "My God! Dunbar is doing this just because I wouldn't sleep with him!"

Def. Att: Objection, hearsay.

14. The Court: Overruled. It's an excited utterance.

Q: Nothing further at this time.

Cross Examination of Martha Olsen by Counsel for Dunbar

15. Q: Ms. Olsen, Mr. Dunbar never made any sexual advances of any kind towards you, isn't that correct?

A: No, he didn't.

Q: You testified earlier that you met at least weekly with Mr. Dunbar to review bookstore operations, right?

A: Yes, usually.

Q: And at a meeting in mid-January, he asked you to institute a new sales procedure by which the salespeople would ask customers to fill out address cards, correct?

A: Yes.

Q: Near the end of January, Mr. Dunbar asked you how the new sales procedure was working out?

A: Yes.

16. Q: And you told him that Susan Palmer was critical of it, and did not always adhere to it?

17. A: I did tell him that, but it's also true that other salespeople objected to it as well.

Q: Your Honor, I ask that everything after "I did tell him that" be stricken as non-responsive and irrelevant.

18. The Court: Yes, that will be stricken.

19. Q: During this meeting, didn't he also tell you that he wanted you to fire Susan Palmer unless she adhered to the sales procedure?

A: No, he didn't say that.

Q: Ms. Olsen, please look at what has previously been marked Exh. D for identification, and see if it refreshes your recollection as to whether Mr. Dunbar made this remark to you during this meeting.

Pl. Att: Objection, Your Honor, as the witness hasn't said she can't remember, there's no basis for refreshing her recollection.

20. The Court: I'll allow counsel to show her the document.

   A: I remember now, he did say that.

   Q: Ms. Olsen, after leaving Mr. Dunbar's bookshop, you went to work for Book Market, didn't you?

   A: Yes.

   Q: But Book Market closed about 6 months later and you lost your job, correct?

   A: That's true.

   Q: You told Joe Tindall, another Book Market employee, that the reason it had to close is that Dunbar opened up one of his trashy bookstores nearby, didn't you?

   Pl. Att: Objection, hearsay.

21. The Court: Overruled.

   A: I did not say that.

   Q: No further questions at this time. But Your Honor, for the record I do intend to call Joe Tindall as a witness to testify that Ms. Olsen did make this remark to him.

   Pl. Att: Objection, collateral issue.

22. The Court: What ruling?

23. Q: One last question. About two months after Ms. Palmer was fired, didn't Mr. Dunbar mention to you that he only fired Ms. Palmer for reasons of poor work performance?

   A: Yes, he did say that.

   Q: Nothing further.

   The Court: Any redirect?

Pl. Att: Just one short matter.

Redirect Examination of Martha Olsen by Counsel for Palmer

Q: Ms. Olsen, when did Mr. Dunbar fire Susan Palmer?

A: It was in late February.

Q: Did Mr. Dunbar at some point terminate the sales procedure you have just been describing?

A: He did.

Q: When was that?

A: Just a couple of months later.

Def. Att: Objection, irrelevant.

24. The Court: What ruling?

Following Martha Olsen's testimony, the plaintiff calls Frank Enstein, an investigator for the State's Equal Employment Opportunity Commission. After testifying to his personal background, Enstein explained his duties with regard to investigating complaints of, among other things, sexual harassment and discrimination. His testimony continues below.

Direct Examination of Frank Enstein by Plaintiff

Q: Please tell us what happened during your meeting of September 22 with Mr. Dunbar.

25. A: Mr. Dunbar stated that he had fired Ms. Palmer because he thought that Ms. Palmer had a drinking problem. He also said that this was the sixth time an employee had claimed that he had discriminated, that he had won every time before and he would win this time.

Q: Then what happened?

A: I showed Mr. Dunbar the EEOC complaint form that Susan Palmer had filled out, which stated that Mr. Dunbar had fired her because she refused to have a sexual relationship with him. He looked it over, and just handed it back to me without saying anything.

Def. Att: Objection and move to strike, hearsay of Palmer.

Pl. Att: Offered as defendant's admission-by-silence.

26. The Court: My task is to determine whether the defendant has convinced me by a preponderance of the evidence that he did not intend to manifest his belief in the truth of the contents of the complaint.

27. The Court: Objection sustained. The answer will be stricken, and I instruct the jury to disregard it.

Q: Did Mr. Dunbar express any views about sexual harassment during your visit with him?

28. A: He said that the law should define sexual harassment as forceful sexual intercourse, and nothing else.

Q: Did he say anything with respect to the Palmer matter?

29. A: As I was leaving he said, "So maybe there was some sexual harassment of that jerk Palmer. Just try to prove it."

Q: Did you speak to anyone else during this same visit?

A: Yes, I spoke to George Harrison, one of the bookstore employees.

Q: What did Mr. Harrison tell you?

30. A: One thing he mentioned was that none of the bookstore's employees consistently followed the sales procedure of getting personal information about each customer, and that Mr. Dunbar knew this.

Q: Where did your conversation with Mr. Harrison take place?

A: Right at the sales counter. I wanted to go to a private office, but Mr. Harrison said that as business was pretty slow we could just talk at the counter.

Def. Att: Objection to what Harrison said as hearsay.

31. The Court: Overruled.

Q: And did you observe anything with respect to the sales procedure while you were at the counter?

32. A: Yes. Mr. Harrison pointed to a customer who was just leaving the store, and said, "See that guy just leaving the store? I just sold him an anthology on The Beatles. I didn't bother to follow the sales procedure with him."

Q: Did he say anything else?

33. A: He mentioned that soon after Susan Palmer was fired, he went up to Mr. Dunbar and said, "You only fired her because she wouldn't sleep with you." In reply to this, Harrison told me that Dunbar said nothing, and after a few seconds just walked away.

Q: Mr. Enstein, how many cases of sexual discrimination would you say you have investigated?

A: I'm sure at least 75-100.

34. Q: Based upon your investigation in this matter, would your opinion be that Ms. Palmer was fired because she would not have sexual relations with Mr. Dunbar?

A: Yes, that is my opinion.

Cross Examination of Frank Enstein by Defense Counsel

Q: Following your meeting with Mr. Dunbar, you spoke with him by phone, correct?

A: I recall that, yes.

35. Q: And didn't he tell you at that time that the only reason he fired Ms. Palmer was for poor work performance?

A: I think he said that.

Q: Prior to your employment with the EEOC, you worked as a securities broker, did you not?

A: I did.

36. Q: But the brokerage firm you were working for fired you for churning clients' accounts-- that is, making excessive trades solely in order to earn commissions?

A: It's true that I was fired, but not for that reason.

Q: For the record, Your Honor, during its case in chief the defense intends to call Bonnie Fide, Mr. Enstein's former supervisor at the brokerage firm, to testify that he was indeed fired for churning.

37. The Court: What ruling?

Chapter 5

Hearsay Exceptions Requiring Unavailability

Transcript 11: "Exceptions Requiring Unavailability" (FRE 804)

A. Background

The hearsay exceptions defined by Rule 804 require the proponent of the assertion to demonstrate that the person who made the statement is "unavailable." The added foundational burden is a sure sign that the drafters were dubious of the reliability of the types of assertions requiring unavailability, but thought that admission was a better alternative than forgoing them altogether.

As used in FRE 804, the term "unavailable" is both overly- and underly-inclusive. On the one hand, a witness may be sitting in court plain as day and still be unavailable. If a witness has a privilege not to testify, has no present recollection of the subject matter of the testimony, or persists in refusing to testify (e.g., as a result of threats), the witness may be both present and unavailable.

On the other hand, it means more than simply, "The witness is not present in court." Your representation that, "I've checked the whole courthouse and can't find Cooper anywhere" is not sufficient to establish Cooper's unavailability. Typically, you must prove that you used "reasonable means" in an effort to find a witness. While reasonableness varies from case to case, something less than the search for Amelia Earhart normally suffices. However, as these exceptions tend to be disfavored, the foundational requirements may be strictly enforced. In one state case, for example, an ex-husband sought to offer hearsay statements by his ex-wife, claiming that she was unavailable. The husband's foundational evidence showed that he had not spoken to her in three years, that a letter he sent to her had been returned undelivered, that her former home had been foreclosed, that five creditors had asked for the ex-husband's help to locate her, that she was not listed in any area phone directory, and that opposing counsel had previously filed an affidavit stating that counsel was unable to locate the ex-wife. The appellate court upheld the trial court's ruling that unavailability of the ex-wife had not been shown. <u>Gordon v. D.G. Escrow Co.</u>, 48 Cal. App. 3d 616, 122 Cal. Rptr. 150 (1975).

The exception for <u>statements against interest</u> is based on the notion that since reasonable people are reluctant to expose themselves to potential civil or criminal liability, a statement that does so may well be accurate. However, it may be difficult to tell that a statement, <u>when made</u>, is against a speaker's interest. Not all cases are as easy as, "I guess it was me who bulldozed the orphanage by mistake." If a speaker says, "I am the lead singer of the Frenchi Vanilli group," a finding as to whether the statement is against the speaker's interest may turn on whether the group has a new hit record or has been charged with fraud for using pre-recorded music in live concerts.

Other foundational difficulties often attend this hearsay exception. A statement against penal interest, offered to exculpate a criminal defendant, is not admissible unless the judge finds that the statement is trustworthy. This requirement reflects the suspicion that criminal defendants would otherwise routinely get their friends to commit perjury by testifying that an unavailable declarant confessed to whatever dastardly deed the defendant is charged with. The requirement converts defendants seeking to offer confessions of absent declarants into prosecutors who must convince the court (by a preponderance of evidence) that the speaker spoke accurately.

(Note that as originally proposed, a statement against interest would have included a statement tending to make the speaker an object of hatred, ridicule or disgrace. Under FRE 804 such statements are not admissible, but they are likely to get a speaker a guest shot on a television talk show.)

Former testimony may also be admissible if a declarant is unavailable. Typical offerings include depositions and testimony during preliminary hearings and retried matters. Since the party against whom the former testimony is offered will not have a chance to question the unavailable speaker whose former testimony is offered, the party must have had an opportunity to do so with a similar motive when the testimony was given, even if the opportunity was not exercised.

The theory behind admitting *statements made under belief of impending death* is plain. Martin lies dying, and with a last breath utters, "Lewis shot me," or "The chicken came first." Surely Martin would not want to go out a liar. Thus, the first statement would be admissible in a prosecution of Lewis for the murder of Martin. Or, if Martin lives but is unavailable, the first statement would be admissible against Lewis in a civil battery action brought by Martin. The key foundational requirement is that the speaker must be aware of imminent death at the time the statement is made. If Martin says, "Lewis is out to get me," in blissful ignorance that a two ton safe is at that very moment 30 feet directly above his head and dropping rapidly, Martin's statement is not admissible.

The Federal Rules admit statements made under a sense of impending death only in civil cases and homicide prosecutions. The latter limitation seems a bit perverse. If such statements are not reliable enough for lesser crimes, why are they reliable enough in homicide cases?

B. *Testimony*

State v. Milhouse

Richard Milhouse is charged with murdering a store clerk in the course of an armed robbery of the Booze Brothers liquor store on Dec. 1. The defense is mistaken identity.

The prosecution's first witness is Alphonso Bedoya. Personal background questioning has concluded.

Direct Examination of Alphonso Bedoya by the Prosecution

    Q: All right, Mr. Bedoya, where were you on the evening of Dec. 1, at about 11:30 P.M.?

    A: I was getting some snacks in the Booze Brothers liquor store.

1. Q: Did you actually see the defendant, that man seated over there, enter the liquor store?

    A: No.

2. Q: When did you realize that a robbery was taking place, and what called your attention to it?

    A: I heard the clerk say that he'd pushed a button to call the police. Then that man over there [indicating the defendant] said, "Badges? You think I'm afraid of a few stinking badges? This is my ninth stickup. Give me the money now, or else."

    Def. Att: Your Honor, I ask permission to question this witness briefly on voir dire to determine whether he has personal knowledge that it was the defendant who made this remark.

    The Court: You may proceed.

Voir Dire Examination of Bedoya by Defense Counsel

3. Q: Mr. Bedoya, at the time you heard the conversation to which you have just testified, you were not looking at the counter, correct?

    A: That's true. I was off to the side, getting some soda.

Q: So you were not looking at whoever made the remark about "stinking badges" at the time it was made?

A: That's true. But I knew it wasn't the clerk who said it because I knew his voice from talking to him before, and when I looked a few seconds later the defendant was the only other person at the counter.

Def. Att: Nothing further. Object and move to strike, lack of personal knowledge.

4. The Court: Prosecution, anything further? No? All right, I needn't be convinced that the defendant made the remark; I can admit it as long as there's evidence from which the jury could reasonably conclude that he said it.

5. The Court: I find the evidence sufficient, and overrule the objection.

Def. Att: Object also, inadmissible hearsay.

6. The Court: That objection is also overruled. Prosecution may continue with the witness' direct examination.

Continued Direct Examination of Bedoya by Prosecution

Q: All right Mr. Bedoya, what happened next?

A: I heard the clerk say something like he wouldn't hand over any money, and that the robber was a jerk who was just bluffing.

Def. Att: Objection, hearsay.

7. Pros: It's not hearsay because the witness paraphrased and did not use the clerk's exact words.

8. The Court: Well, I agree it's non-hearsay,

> I'll allow it.

9. Q: Thank you, Your Honor. Mr. Bedoya, what next occurred?

10. A: I heard two quick pops. Based on how they sounded, I'd say they were gunshots.

    Q: Then what happened?

    A: The next thing I knew I heard someone running towards the door, and the door slammed back. I figured it was the robber running out of the door, so I went towards the counter to check on the clerk.

    Q: Did you hear anything before you reached the counter?

11. A: Yes. From somewhere towards the back of the store I heard someone yell, "Hurry-- call the cops. They can catch him if they hurry-- the robber runs with a big limp.

    Q: Did you then check on the clerk?

    A: Yes. It was terrible. He was lying down all crumpled up. There was blood all over his shirt and on the floor, and he could hardly breathe. I held his hand to try to comfort him, and that's when I heard him whisper, "The guy who did this tried to rob me once before. You can't mistake him; he's got a big scar on his forehead. I think he knew all along he was going to shoot me."

    Q: Did you hear him say anything else?

    A: He said something about hoping to make it, but then he collapsed. That's the last I heard.

    Def. Att: Objection and move to strike everything the clerk said as hearsay;

there's no evidence that the statement was made under a sense of impending death.

12. The Court: I am to admit the statement unless I find by a preponderance of the evidence that it was not made under a sense of impending death.

13. The Court: I'll admit everything except "The guy who did this tried to rob me once before." That statement is stricken.

   Q: Did you say anything to the clerk?

14. A: I wasn't sure he could hear me, but I told him that a person in the back of the store got a good look at who did it.

   Q: Nothing further.

Cross Examination of Bedoya by Defense Counsel

   Q: Mr. Bedoya, a couple of weeks ago you spoke to a man by the name of Johnson about this incident, right?

   A: That's right, I did.

15. Q: And didn't he tell you that he was the one who had done the Dec. 1 liquor store robbery, and that Milhouse was the wrong guy?

   A: Something like that.

16. Q: And at an office party about a month ago, didn't you say to a co-worker, "Even if I have to commit perjury, I'm going to help convict that guy for the liquor store holdup."

   A: Well, I had had a few drinks, I didn't mean it.

   Pros: Move to strike the question and answer, as the witness' answer indicates that since he had been drinking the remark is unworthy of serious consideration.

17. The Court: What ruling?

   Q: Nothing further.

   Pros: Our next witness is the arresting officer, Off. Barb Wire.

Direct Examination of Off. Wire by Prosecution

   Q: Off. Wire, are you the arresting officer in this case?

   A: I am. I arrested Mr. Milhouse at approximately 11:45 on Dec. 1.

   Q: Did you speak to him shortly after his arrest?

   A: I did.

18. Q: And prior to speaking to him, did you advise him of his <u>Miranda</u> rights?

   A: I did.

   Q: How did he respond?

19. A: He agreed to speak to me.

   Def. Att: Your Honor, I ask permission to call the defendant to testify solely to the foundational issue of the waiver of his <u>Miranda</u> rights. The defendant does not otherwise waive his privilege not to testify.

20. The Court: That is permissible; I'll allow it. The jury may remain.

Voir Dire Examination of Defendant by Defense Counsel

   Q: Mr. Milhouse, do you recall speaking to Off. Wire shortly after your arrest?

   A: I do.

Q: Prior to talking to you, did she tell you you had a right to speak to an attorney before answering any questions?

A: No.

Q: Are you sure?

21. A: Yes. A little later, I told my cellmate, Steven Even, that since she hadn't given me my rights, nothing I told her could be used against me.

Q: Nothing further.

Pros: No questions. I recall Off. Wire.

Direct Examination of Off. Wire by Prosecution

Q: Officer, prior to questioning Mr. Milhouse, what did you tell him?

A: That he had a right to remain silent, to consult with a lawyer before talking to me, that if he could not afford an attorney one could be appointed for him, and that if he talked to me, whatever he said could be used in court.

Q: How did he respond?

A: He said he wanted to speak to me.

22. The Court: I find that Mr. Milhouse validly waived his constitutional rights, but I instruct the jury to disregard anything the defendant might have said to the officer if the jurors believe that there was no valid waiver.

Q: Now, Off. Wire, what did Mr. Milhouse tell you concerning the liquor store robbery?

23. A: He said he hadn't done anything, that he hadn't been anywhere near the store that night.

Q: What else occurred?

24. A: I said, "Come on, Milhouse, you know you did it." He just stared at the floor and never said another word.

Q: Nothing further.

<u>Cross Examination of Off. Wire by Defense Counsel</u>

Q: Off. Wire, isn't it true that two years ago, Mr. Milhouse filed a complaint with the police department accusing you of using unlawful force when arresting him on a traffic warrant?

Pros: Objection, beyond the scope of direct.

25. The Court: Overruled.

A: That's correct, but I was exonerated.

26. Q: And last year, weren't you suspended by the Police Commission for one month for using excessive force to make an arrest?

A: Yes.

Q: No further questions.

Following Off. Wire's testimony, the prosecution informs the court that it wishes to enter into the record the testimony of a witness who testified at Milhouse's preliminary hearing, Ben Dover. According to the prosecutor, Dover is physically present in court, but "unavailable" because he has received threats from Milhouse and refuses to testify. The prosecution first attempts to lay a foundation establishing that Dover is unavailable. If the judge finds that Dover is unavailable, the prosecution will then seek to enter his testimony at the preliminary hearing into the record.

<u>Voir Dire Examination of Ben Dover by Prosecution</u>

Def. Att: Before proceeding, I'd ask that the jury be excused during this testimony.

27. The Court: It's within my discretion, and to save time we'll keep the jury here.

Q: Mr. Dover, you recall testifying at the preliminary hearing in this matter?

A: Yes, I testified.

Q: Did you later receive any telephone calls concerning that testimony?

A: Yes, about four days later someone, I think it was Milhouse, called and said I'm a dead man if I testify against him in court. He said he knew where I lived and work, and had plenty of friends who wouldn't mind doing a small job for him if necessary.

Q: What tone of voice did he use?

28. A: A low, kind of menacing tone of voice.

29. Q: How can you be so sure it was Milhouse?

A: Well, based on hearing him talk when I was here for the prelim.

Q: Did he use the tone that you described as low and menacing at the prelim?

A: No.

Q: And had you ever heard him speak before?

A: No, but there was just a tone to the voice that makes me think it was him on the phone.

Q: Mr. Dover, are you willing to testify here at trial?

A: No way. A friend told me about a TV show he saw that talked about some recent death threats against witnesses that were carried out. I'm sorry. I don't care if you put me in jail, I'm not testifying.

Def. Att: Objection to what the friend said about the TV show, double hearsay.

30. The Court: I admit it as non-hearsay.

31. The Court: Even if it's offered for its truth, the objection is overruled.

The Court: Mr. Dover, you have a duty to testify to any matter that may help us determine Mr. Mihouse's guilt or innocence, and I order you to do so.

A: I understand all that. But I got that telephone call, you didn't, and I'm not testifying.

The Court: Anything further?

Def. Att: I'd object to the use of the witness' testimony at the preliminary hearing. In view of my client's constitutional right to confront witnesses, Your Honor should postpone the trial and consider putting the witness in jail for contempt of court before allowing use of the earlier testimony.

32. The Court: I think the foundation is adequate to show unavailability. Are the other requirements of FRE 804(b)(1) met?

Pros: Dover was called by the prosecutor,

and he stated that he was about to enter the liquor store in question when he heard two gunshots. He then saw someone rush past him, and identified Milhouse as that person. Mr. Milhouse was represented by other counsel at the prelim.; that defense counsel waived cross.

Def. Att: I'd object, based in part on the absence of cross, and in part on the fact that at the time of the preliminary hearing, the clerk was still in hospital and the charge was attempted murder. The clerk has since died, and Mr. Milhouse is now charged with murder. In view of the serious nature of the charges, the change in charges, and the absence of cross examination at the preliminary hearing, it would be unfair to allow introduction of Dover's earlier testimony.

33. The Court: What ruling?

After the prosecution rested, Milhouse was called as a witness in his own defense.

Direct Examination of Milhouse by Defense Counsel

Q: Mr. Milhouse, on Dec. 1, did you rob the Booze Brothers liquor store and shoot the clerk?

34. A: No. I've never shot or killed anyone.

Q: Were you at the liquor store that night?

A: I had been in there to pick up a few snacks a few minutes before all hell broke loose. A friend of mine had called and said he'd gotten a card game together, so I should walk over to the liquor store and get some snacks and he'd pick me up around 11:30. So I was standing outside with the snacks when I heard the gunshots.

Pros: Objection to what the friend said, hearsay.

35. The Court: Overruled.

    Q: What is the name of this friend?

    A: Stan Dupp.

    Q: Is Mr. Dupp here to testify?

    A: No, he can't get off work to be here.

    Pros: Objection, that's an insufficient showing of FRE 804 unavailability.

36. The Court: Overruled, the answer and the testimony may stand.

    Q: After your arrest by Off. Wire, you were placed in custody, correct?

    A: Yes.

    Q: While you were in jail, did you have a discussion with anyone concerning the Dec. 1 incident at the Booze Brothers liquor store?

    A: Yes, with Fred Cooper, who was in the next cell.

    Q: When did this conversation take place?

    A: I remember it was the night of Dec. 5.

    Q: And what did Mr. Cooper tell you?

    Pros: Objection, hearsay.

    Def. Att: The statement will be offered as Cooper's declaration against interest.

37. The Court: In that case, the defense must offer evidence sufficient for a jury to find reasonably that Cooper is unavailable. Proceed.

    Q: Mr. Milhouse, do you know where Mr. Cooper is?

A: Not the slightest idea. He told me he had some relations in Boise is all I know. He got out just a few days after he talked to me, and that's the last I saw him.

Q: Your Honor, on the foundation issue, I next call Paul Dreck.

Voir Dire Examination of Paul Dreck by Defense Counsel

Q: Mr. Dreck, how are you employed?

A: I'm a licensed private investigator.

38. Q: And did I employ you to attempt to locate the Fred Cooper who was released from the County Jail on or about Dec. 10?

A: You did.

Q: Please describe your efforts to do so.

A: Certainly. I first checked Sheriff Department records; they indicated that Cooper had been released on Dec. 10. He gave his address as the Bates Motel, but when I called the motel the manager told me she had no record of a Fred Cooper.

Pros: Objection to the manager's statement, hearsay. Move to strike.

39. The Court: Overruled.

Q: Please continue.

A: I thought he might have registered under a different name, so I went by the Bates Motel with a photo I had gotten from Sheriff's records. No one there recognized him.

Q: Anything else that you did?

A: Well, the usual. I checked with the various utility companies, and with his only known relative here, a cousin named Aura Cooper Berg. Based on what Mr. Milhouse told me, I also checked with authorities in Boise, as well as utility records there. I was not able to locate Mr. Cooper through any of these sources. Altogether, I spent about 15 hours in the search on five different days.

Def. Att: We'll submit it, Your Honor.

40. The Court: Prosecution wish to question? No questions? In that case, I rule that Cooper is unavailable. Defense may proceed; defendant may resume the stand.

Continued Direct Examination of Milhouse by Defense Counsel

Q: All right, Mr. Milhouse, what did Mr. Cooper tell you the evening of Dec. 5?

A: He asked what I was in for, and I told him for robbing the Booze Brothers store shooting the clerk. I said I was innocent, that I was at the store just waiting for a ride when I heard some shots and ran so I wouldn't get shot, and that's when I was arrested. Then Cooper said...

Pros: Move to strike the defendant's statement as hearsay.

41. The Court: Sustained.

Q: Please tell us what Cooper told you.

A: He said, "I know you're innocent; I saw you standing outside the store when I ran by. I'm the one who did it. I bet they'll cut you loose in a day or two." Then he took out a piece of paper, it was a receipt from some jewelry store. I only remember the date, Dec. 2. He said he had bought a diamond ring with the loot and had mailed it to a post office box

88

where the authorities would never find it.

Def. Att: Your Honor, the prosecution has agreed to stipulate that on Dec. 2, Linda Able, owner of Crescent Jewelers, sold a two carat diamond ring to Mr. Fred Cooper.

Pros: That's correct.

42. The Court: Under the circumstances, I admit Mr. Cooper's statement under 804(b)(3).

Q: How did you respond?

43. A: I said, "My God. I can prove that I'm innocent."

Q: Nothing further.

Chapter 6

Character Evidence

Transcript 12: "Character To Prove Conduct" (FRE 404, 405)

A. Background

The Federal Rules of Evidence make character evidence potentially admissible in three different situations, and potentially provable through three different methods. Thus, centuries of experience with character evidence have provided symmetry, if not clarity. This superficial neatness should not obscure the fact that character evidence is often the most controversial form of evidence a party can offer. In general, the Rules admit character evidence the way most of us admit our shortcomings-- with great reluctance.

One situation in which character evidence is potentially admissible is when it is offered as circumstantial evidence of <u>conduct on a particular occasion</u>. For example, evidence of Jean's pacifist nature may be offered as circumstantial evidence that Jean did not commit a violent crime. From evidence of a trait of Jean's character (pacifism) the trier of fact is asked to infer how Jean behaved (did not commit a violent act).

A second situation in which character evidence is potentially admissible is when it is offered as circumstantial evidence to support or attack a witness' <u>credibility</u>. For example, evidence that Jean has a propensity to tell lies might be offered to prove that Jean is not telling the truth on the witness stand.

(Note that first two situations overlap somewhat. In each case, character evidence is offered as circumstantial evidence of behavior. In the first situation, however, the behavior to which the character evidence pertains occurs out of court, and the character evidence varies according to the conduct at issue in each case.

In the second the behavior always concerns either lying or truthtelling, and that behavior occurs in court, on the witness stand.)

The third situation in which character evidence is potentially admissible is when it is offered as direct evidence of a character trait which itself an <u>ultimate issue</u> ("material fact"). For instance, evidence that Jean has a propensity to tell lies might be offered by Jan in a slander case in which Jean has sued Jan for saying that "Jean is a liar of the worst stripe." Jean's character as a truthteller would be an ultimate issue, and evidence of Jean's honest or dishonest character would therefore constitute direct evidence.

When character evidence is admissible, it can be potentially proved by three different types of evidence: specific acts, opinion and reputation evidence. Except for the rare litigant who has acquired a reputation by having his/her face and other assorted body parts displayed on the cover of supermarket tabloids, parties often try to prove character through evidence of <u>specific acts</u>. For example, to prove that Jean is a pacifist, Jean might offer evidence that on specific occasions when Jean was challenged to a fight, Jean walked away. To attack Jean's credibility through specific acts evidence, a party might offer evidence that Jean has been convicted of perjury. Lastly, to prove Jean's honesty in the slander action against Jan through a specific act, Jean might offer evidence of finding a wallet containing $10,000 and turning it immediately in to the police. Because specific acts evidence involves peripheral activities, it tends to be time consuming. Also, it is doubtful that an inference of character may be drawn legitimately from the few isolated peripheral acts a court takes the time to admit into evidence. Hence, both the Federal Rules and judicial discretion often take a dim view of a party's attempt to offer specific acts evidence.

When a party seeks to offer <u>opinion</u> character evidence, a witness who is personally acquainted with a party testifies that in the witness' personal opinion, the party does or does not possess a particular character trait. For example, to prove that Jean is a pacifist, Jean might offer testimony from Jean's best friend of 15 years that in the friend's opinion, Jean is a peaceful person who would not harm a fly. Similarly, to attack Jean's credibility, the opposing party might offer testimony from someone with whom Jean has worked for years that in the coworker's opinion, Jean is dishonest.

Character evidence in the form of <u>reputation</u> consists of a witness' testifying to what a party's friends or coworkers say about the party. For example, to prove that Jean is a pacifist, Jean might offer testimony from Jean's supervisor at work that Jean has a reputation as a peaceful person who would not harm a fly. Likewise, to attack Jean's credibility, the opposing party might offer evidence of someone who has been in the same bowling league as Jean for years that Jean's has a reputation for being dishonest. Reputation evidence obviously involves hearsay. But the Federal Rules provide an exception in Rule 803 (19), thereby reflecting the view that while an isolated hearsay statement may not be trustworthy, an accumulation of the stuff is worth listening to.

The character evidence rules assume that each of us is a bundle of independent traits of character. We might be honest yet violent, sober in our investment strategy yet reckless in our driving. Thus, when character evidence is admissible, the character trait of which evidence is offered must be the precise one in issue. One cannot offer evidence that someone is honest, and from that ask the trier of fact to infer that the person also is punctual.

The above discussion of character evidence rules has managed to miss what is frequently the most subtle, interesting and important aspect of character evidence: is proffered evidence character evidence, or is it relevant on a non-character theory? To take a simple example, assume that Jean is on trial for murder, and an eyewitness testifies, "I saw Jean shoot the victim." Can Jean's attorney exclude the evidence with an argument such as, "We can't admit that. The jurors will think Jean a terrible person if they hear that." Of course not. The evidence is relevant without regard to Jean's character. That is, regardless of whether Jean has a propensity towards violence, the testimony suggests that Jean engaged in the charged conduct.

But in other situations, the answer is not so clear. To take a non-judicial example that got wide public attention, recall the 1991 Senate confirmation hearings on the nomination of Judge Clarence Thomas to the United States Supreme Court. During the hearings, Professor Anita Hill testified that some years earlier, when both she and Judge Thomas were working in the same government agency, Judge Thomas had made a number of unwelcome sexual advances towards her. Opponents of the Thomas nomination then attempted to offer testimony from other coworkers that Judge Thomas had also made sexual advances towards them. If the only relevance of the coworkers' testimony was to show that Judge Thomas had a propensity to make sexual advances, it would have been excluded in a court of law.

But might the testimony have been relevant on a non-character theory? The answer often depends on identifying with precision the disputed issues in a specific case. For example, assume hypothetically that Judge Thomas' defense had been that he did make sexual remarks to Prof. Hill, but that they were not sexual advances. Rather, the remarks were necessary to a discussion of a sexual discrimination case being handled by the agency for which both Thomas and Hill were working. (During the Senate confirmation hearings, Judge Thomas' actual defense was a denial that he made any sexual remarks to Prof. Hill whatsoever.) In this hypothetical example, evidence from other co-workers that Judge Thomas made sexual remarks to them might be relevant on a non-character theory. The evidence might disprove the claim that Judge Hill made sexual remarks only pursuant to discussion of sexual discrimination cases.

B. <u>Testimony</u>

<u>Mentry v. McSoftware Corp.</u>

This is a civil dispute in which plaintiff Ella Mentry sues to recover damages for fraud and breach of contract; the complaint seeks actual and punitive damages, as well as attorneys' fees. Mentry contends that she was hired as an independent contractor on June 1 by Marcus Nieman, the president and sole owner of defendant McSoftware, to develop a litigation support system. According to Mentry, the term of the contract was 6 months; she was to be paid $55,000. Relying on the agreement, Mentry quit her previous place of employment and moved to the state of McSoftware's principal place of business. When she reported for work on July 1, however, she was told by Nieman that McSoftware was no longer interested in her services. Mentry contends that Nieman defrauded her into leaving her job and moving out of state.

McSoftware's defense is that its failure to hire Mentry was due entirely to changed market conditions rendering unfeasible development of a litigation support program, and that Nieman told Mentry that while McSoftware was interested in employing her, no final job offer could be made until July 1.

The first witness is the plaintiff, Ella Mentry.

Direct Examination of Plaintiff Ella Mentry

Q: Ms. Mentry, what is your occupation?

A: I'm a computer programmer. I develop software programs for use in microcomputers.

Q: How long have you been in this line of work?

A: Since graduation from college, about 12 years.

1. Q: Are you active in any civic organizations?

A: Yes, I'm a volunteer docent at the County Art Museum. My husband and I also sponsor a child through Foster Parents Plan.

2. Q: Please tell us about events that culminated in defendant's agreement to hire you on June 1 to develop a litigation support system.

   A: (Mentry testifies to working as a programmer at Software King, responding to a McSoftware ad in a trade magazine, talking to Marcus over the phone and in person, being offered the job, accepting, and being told by Marcus to start work on July 1.)

   Q: Did you report to work on July 1?

   A: I did.

   Q: And what happened?

   A: I was shown into Mr. Marcus' office. He told me that my services were no longer needed.

   Def. Att: Objection, hearsay.

3. The Court: Overruled, it goes to state of mind.

   Q: Did Mr. Marcus do anything else during this meeting?

   A: Yes. He handed me a piece of paper and asked me to sign it.

4. Q: What did this piece of paper say?

   A: It said that I recognized that I had not been offered a job by McSoftware, and that I had quit my former employment of my own volition.

   Q: Did you sign this piece of paper?

   A: Certainly not.

   Q: All right. What else happened?

A: Nieman told me that I was the second Software King employee he had tricked into leaving the company.

Q: Did he explain this?

5. A: Yes. He said that a year earlier he had made a phony job offer to another Software King employee, John Golyer. He ran the same kind of ad I saw, but told all applicants except Golyer that the position had been filled. He said he knew that Golyer's specialty was medical practice software, so he told Golyer that McSoftware needed someone to develop that kind of software. Then, when Golyer showed up to work Nieman told him that changed market conditions meant McSoftware could not go ahead with the program, and that Golyer had no claim because he would say that he had told Golyer that no definite offer could have been made until McSoftware completed a market survey.

Q: Did Nieman say why he had done this to you and Golyer?

6. A: Yes, I asked him about that. He told me that he had been fired by Software King about 6 years earlier for pirating some programs they had developed, and that he was simply getting back the best way he could.

Q: During this conversation, did Nieman say anything to you about McSoftware's marketing of a software program by the name of Wirdpurfeck?

A: Yes. He said that this was a spell-check program that the company had designed, and that since it was aimed at individual users who would not know enough to complain, it was his suggestion that McSoftware should make exaggerated claims for the program to induce purchasers to buy it.

Def. Att: Objection, Your Honor, lack of foundation and inadmissible character evidence.

7. The Court: As to foundation, I merely have to find that the evidence is sufficient to support the jury's finding that Mr. Nieman did make this statement.

8. The Court: But I will sustain the objection as to character evidence. The witness' last answer will be stricken.

Q: (Remainder of examination omitted)

Cross Examination by Defense Counsel

Q: Ms. Mentry, you had had some dealings with Mr. Nieman before this incident, isn't that correct?

A: Just briefly.

Q: Well, before going to work for Software King you had applied to Mr. Nieman for a job with McSoftware, isn't that true?

A: Yes, that's right.

Q: And he told you that he had rejected you because you had falsified information about your college record, correct?

Pl. Att: Objection, Your Honor. Improper character evidence.

9. The Court: Well, as a witness her character is in issue.

10. The Court: I'll also admit it for a non-character use.

A: He may have.

11. Q: The truth is that he did tell you that, isn't it?

A: Yes.

12. Q: During the time you were working at Software King, you were put on probation by the company for submitting falsified health insurance claims, were you not?

A: Just the one time.

Q: Now, Ms. Mentry, you knew when you decided to show up at McSoftware's office on July 1 that Mr. Nieman had not promised you a job, isn't that correct?

A: That is definitely not correct. As I testified earlier, he agreed to hire me during a conversation on June 1.

Q: And when you appeared in Mr. Nieman's office on July 1, you asked for an immediate advance on your salary, isn't that true?

A: Yes, I did. Moving expenses were a bit higher than I had anticipated.

13. Q: Isn't it true that the real reason you asked for an advance, and that you claim that Mr. Nieman had agreed to hire you, is that Software King discovered you had stolen some of its property just before you left, and you were in desperate need of money to pay it back?

A: No.

Def. Att: No further questions at this time.

Pl. Att: No redirect. At this time the plaintiff calls its next witness, Alice Tarecook.

Direct Examination of Alice Tarecook by Plaintiff

(Preliminary questioning omitted)

Q: Ms. Tarecook, do you know the defendant in this matter, Mr. Nieman?

A: I do. We've served together on a number of computer industry trade association committees.

Q: How often do you see him?

A: Over the course of the last 5 or 6 years, at least once a month, sometimes more often than that.

Q: How well have you gotten to know him?

A: Very well; we've talked about computer business problems frequently.

14. Q: Do you have an opinion as to whether Mr. Nieman is an honest and trustworthy individual?

A: Yes. I do not regard him as an honest person.

Q: Have you also spoken to other people on these trade association committees about Mr. Nieman?

A: I have.

15. Q: And does he have a reputation as far as honesty and trustworthiness goes?

A: Yes. He's regarded as a dishonest businessperson.

Transcript 13: "Character to Prove Conduct"
(FRE 404, 405)

A. Background

See also, discussion accompanying Transcript 12.

The Federal Rules, unlike everyday life, force us to distinguish between people's propensities and their habits. The obstacles that the Rules place in front of character evidence become welcome mats for evidence of habit. See FRE 406. A variety of reasons support this differential attitude. First, habits are limited forms of behavior, consisting of regular responses to specific situations. Thus, regardless of whether one has a propensity to drive carefully (a character trait), one may habitually stop at the stop sign at the intersection of Elm and Rodeo Drives.

Moreover, because habits are observable, witnesses who provide habit testimony can be examined and cross examined to the same extent as other witnesses. That is, a witness who testifies that, "Bergman tugs at his ear every 45 seconds," provides objectively verifiable data (at least, data which is as objectively verifiable as any other) and can be cross examined to the same extent as other percipient witnesses. By contrast, witnesses who provide their opinions of peoples' characters necessarily deliver subjective judgments which always remain to some extent impervious to cross.

Finally, habit is largely free of the moralistic overtones that often accompany character evidence. The character traits likely to be relevant in litigation-- violence, deceit, etc.-- tend to focus on people's moral goodness. While we often think of habits as "good" or "bad," they are typically free of character's moralistic baggage.

B. Testimony

State v. Edwards

Defendant Eddie Edwards is charged with rape. During the prosecution's case-in-chief, Bea Dalton testified that she spoke with Edwards at a party on April 2, accepted his offer to drive her home and allowed him to enter her Hanley Drive apartment to make a telephone call. He then smoked what she thought was a marijuana cigarette, and engaged her in small talk for nearly an hour. Edwards finally left around 11 P.M., but a few minutes later someone jumped through her living room window and attacked her. She screamed. The attacker raped her, then bound her hands and eyes. She heard the attacker rummaging through her bedroom dresser. Though she was crying, she was able to hear the attacker humming the theme to "Bridge Over the River Kwai." After a few moments, the door to her apartment slammed, and everything was quiet. Dalton is pretty sure that the person who jumped through her living room window and attacked her was the defendant Edwards. Three nights after the attack, a number of shots were fired into her living room at about 1:30 A.M. Because of that, she moved in temporarily with a friend.

NOTE: Edwards' defense is a denial that he had sexual relations with Dalton. He contends that he accompanied her into her apartment and left at once.

Following Dalton's testimony, the State announced its intention to call two additional witnesses, Annie Wunholm and Al Falfa. Pursuant to defense counsel's request, the Court agreed to take Wunholm's and Falfa's testimony out of the presence of the jury. After hearing the testimony, the Court will rule on its admissibility. If the Court determines that Wunholm's and/or Falfa's testimony is admissible, the permitted testimony will be re-elicited in front of the jury. However, you should respond to the numbered excerpts as though the testimony below were being offered into evidence.

<u>Direct Examination of Annie Wunholm by Prosecutor</u>

(Preliminary questioning omitted)

Q: Ms. Wunholm, are you acquainted with the defendant Edwards?

A: I am. We lived together for about a year.

Q: Over what period of time did you live together?

A: From September of 2 years ago through October of last year.

1. Q: Did you have any hesitancy with having the defendant move in with you?

2. A: Yes. I had heard that he had been violent with a previous girlfriend. But he assured me that that was all in the past.

3. Q: How would you characterize the nature of your relationship?

A: Most of the time it was OK, but we had problems.

Q: Can you briefly describe those problems for us please.

4. A: About 5 or 6 different times, he hit me. Almost always, it was when he had been drinking after work.

Q: Was there ever a time that he hit you after smoking marijuana?

5. A: Yes. A couple of times I remember him hitting me, and afterwards I asked him why. He said he was sorry, that he didn't know why. He said he'd just smoked a couple of joints, and he figured that would relax him but it didn't.

Q: Ms. Wunholm, were there occasions when you and the defendant were living together that you made love?

A: Yes.

Q: Can you estimate how often?

A: I really can't say for sure. Even though he hit me, we had many good times together. I'd have to say over the year period, at least a 100 times.

Q: Can you tell us if the defendant regularly engaged in any particular behavior after you and he made love?

6. A: He'd hum a funny little tune.

Q: Can you tell us whether the defendant always hummed this tune?

7. A: Well, I can't say always. But almost always.

Q: Do you know the name of this tune?

8. A: I asked him once; he said it was the "Bridge Over the River Kwai," or something like that.

Q: If you're able to, can you hum the tune that the defendant used to hum after you made love?

A: (Witness hums.)

Pros: Your Honor, I request that the court take judicial notice that the witness is humming the theme song to "Bridge Over the River Kwai."

9. The Court: I will take judicial notice of that fact.

Q: Ms. Wunholm, I'd like to call your attention to an incident that took place in early December, a couple of months after you and the defendant stopped living together. Do you know the incident to which I'm referring?

A: I think I do.

Q: Where did the incident take place?

A: In my apartment, about 2:00 in the morning.

Q: Please tell us what happened?

A: I was asleep in my bed when I was awakened by a noise. I saw someone standing near me, and said something like, "who's there." The person grabbed the covers of the bed and shoved them over my face. Then he raped me.

Q: Do you know the identity of the person who attacked you?

A: I couldn't see his face, but after he raped me I could hear him humming that "Bridge Over the River Kwai" tune.

Q: Did you recognize the humming?

A: It sounded like Eddie, if that's what you mean.

Q: Do you know how the attacker entered your apartment?

A: As he was humming that tune I heard him leave by my living room window. The only door to my apartment was still locked afterwards, as were the other windows, so he must have come in through the living room window too.

Pros: This completes our foundational showing, and I ask that the witness be permitted to testify before the jury.

Def. Att: I object to any testimony by this witness concerning a rape in December on the ground that there is insufficient evidence that the defendant Edwards was her attacker.

10. The Court: I can admit the testimony over that objection as long as there is sufficient evidence from which the jury can reasonably conclude that

Edwards was the person who raped her in early December.

11. The Court: I overrule that objection; there is sufficient evidence that the attacker was Edwards.

Def. Att: I also object on the ground that evidence of the rape would constitute improper character evidence.

12. The Court: What ruling?

Pros: Continuing with the preliminary questioning, Your Honor, the State next calls Al Falfa to the witness stand.

<u>Direct Examination of Al Falfa by the Prosecutor</u>

(Preliminary questioning omitted)

Q: Mr. Falfa, how do you know the defendant, Eddie Edwards?

A: We have some friends in common, I guess you'd say. I see him sometimes at parties, maybe down at the tavern, that sort of thing.

13. Q: Have you ever known Edwards to engage in unlawful sexual conduct?

A: I wouldn't know anything about that.

Q: Do you recall being in the company of Edwards on the night of April 5?

A: Yeah, I was with him.

Q: For the record, Your Honor, this witness is testifying pursuant to a grant of immunity from my office. Mr. Falfa, please tell us what occurred on the night of April 5.

14. A: Well, Eddie came into the tavern around 8 and told me he had had some problems with a girl a couple of nights earlier.

Q: Did you ask him what kind of problems?

A: No.

Q: All right, then what happened?

A: He asked if I had a car because he needed a ride. I did, so we drove around a little and ended up over on Hanley Drive. Eddie asked me to stop in front of one of the apartments, then he took out a gun and shot out one of the windows in a ground floor apartment. Then we drove away.

Q: Could you describe this gun?

A: It was a .38.

Q: And what time was it when Edwards shot out the windows?

A: 1, 1:30 in the morning, somewhere around there.

Pros: Nothing further.

Def. Att: Object as improper character evidence. The only relevance is to depict Mr. Edwards as a violent person.

15. The Court: What ruling?

Q: One last question, Mr. Falfa. Based upon your contacts with the defendant, do you have an opinion as to whether he is a violent person?

16. A: Yes, in my opinion he is very violent.

Q: Nothing further at this time.

Following whatever portion of Wunholm's and Falfa's testimony the Court permitted to be received, the prosecution rested its case. The defense then had the opportunity to present its case in chief, and called the defendant as its first witness. Edwards testified that on the evening of April 2 he attended a party where he met Bea Dalton. He had to leave by 9:30 P.M., because he is a construction worker and had to be at a job site about an hour away from his home by 6 A.M. and thus wanted to be in bed by 10 P.M. When he mentioned this to Dalton, she said she was not feeling well and asked him to drop her off. He did so, and immediately went home and went to sleep by 10 P.M. He never entered Dalton's apartment, and had no sexual contact with her.

The defense then called Bryce Miller as its next witness.

<u>Direct Examination of Bryce Miller by Defense Counsel</u>

(Introductory questions omitted)

Q: Mr. Miller, how long have you known Mr. Edwards?

A: Somewhere between 3-4 years.

Q: And how often have you seen him over that period of time?

A: Sometimes every day, sometimes not for a few weeks. When you're in construction like we are, sometimes there's lots of work, and sometimes you don't work for a few days or even longer.

Q: Do you consider him a close friend?

A: Definitely.

Q: Do you have an opinion as to whether Mr. Edwards is an honest, trustworthy person?

17. A: In my opinion, he is extremely honest and trustworthy.

Q: Can you give us an example of what you mean?

18. A: Yes, Eddie found a wallet with about $500 in it at a house remodeling job

we were doing. He returned the wallet to the owner, money and all.

Q: Does Mr. Edwards have a reputation with respect for honesty among his co-workers?

A: He sure does.

Q: And what is that reputation?

19. A: He's known as a very honest person.

Q: Do you also have an opinion as to whether Mr. Edwards is a peaceable individual?

A: I do.

Q: And what is that opinion?

20. A: My opinion is that he is a peaceful person.

Q: Do you know of anyone else in particular who shares that opinion?

21. A: I know that our construction boss, Ari Catlin, has often told me that he's glad to have a quiet, non-violent guy like Eddie on the job.

Q: What is the basis of your opinion that he's peaceful?

22. A: Some of the guys often start pushing each other around, especially if they've had a few beers after work. Eddie always tries to get them to break it up.

Q: Mr. Miller, did you talk with Mr. Edwards on April 2, the night of the alleged attack on Ms. Dalton?

A: I did.

Q: Where did this conversation take place?

A: Over the phone. I called him to remind him to be out at the Mandeville job site by 6 A.M.

Q: How did Mr. Edwards respond?

A: He said that he had a party he had to show up at, but that he would leave it early and get to sleep by 10:00.

Pros: Objection, hearsay.

23. The Court: Overruled.

Q: You testified earlier that you've worked with Mr. Edwards for 3-4 years. During this time, have you ever lived together?

A: Yes, we lived together for about 3 months when I was hurt and couldn't work.

Q: When was that?

A: I moved out of his place almost a year ago.

Q: During the time you lived with Mr. Edwards, were there times when he had to leave his apartment by 5 A.M. to arrive at a distant job site?

A: Yeah, in our business that's not unusual.

Q: About how often would you say he had to get up at 5 A.M.

24. A: That's pretty hard to say. Just as a guess, I'd say 15-20 times.

Q: When he had to be up at 5 A.M., did he regularly go to bed the night before at any particular time?

Pros: Objection, lack of foundation. There's no showing that this witness has personal knowledge of what time the defendant went to bed.

25. The Court: Sustained.

    Q: For foundation then, Mr. Miller, did you and Mr. Edwards share the same room when you lived together?

    A: No, I slept in the living room.

26. Q: Yet you are confident that you know when he went to sleep?

    A: Oh, yes. When he had to get up early, he'd always say so and tell me he was going to sleep, and go into his room.

Pros: Objection, hearsay.

27. The Court: Overruled.

    Q: When he'd go into his room, would he always go right to sleep?

28. A: Yes, he'd never read, and he had no TV in there. He'd just always go right to sleep.

Def. Att: Nothing further by way of foundation, Your Honor.

29. The Court: I should admit testimony as to the defendant's regular time of going to bed when he had to get up at 5 A.M. even if I have my own doubts, as long as there's sufficient evidence for the jury to find that this witness has personal knowledge of that time.

30. The Court: The foundation is sufficient. I'll allow the witness to answer.

    Q: I'll ask you again, Mr. Miller, what time Mr. Miller would go to bed when he had to be up the next morning at 5 A.M.

31. A: He'd always be in bed by 10.

    Q: Has he continued to follow this pattern since you moved out?

32. A: He's told me that he has.

    Q: No further questions at this time.

    The Court: Cross examination?

Cross Examination of Bryce Miller by the Prosecutor

33. Q: Mr. Miller, are you aware that 2 years ago, the defendant had to pay a penalty for the IRS for underreporting his income tax liability for 3 years?

    A: Yes, I know about that.

    Q: Well, did you know that just last week the defendant was arrested for battery on a police officer?

    Def. Att: Objection, the witness only gave his opinion and cannot be asked about specific acts.

34. The Court: Objection overruled.

    Def. Att: I also object that the witness cannot be asked about arrests, only convictions.

35. The Court: I'll overrule that objection as well.

    Def. Att: I object further that the incident with which the defendant is charged occurred over two months ago; the witness cannot be asked about an occurrence that took place last week.

36. The Court: Well, it's near enough in time. Overruled.

    Def. Att: Lastly, I object that opposing counsel lacks a good faith basis for the question.

    The Court: (To the Prosecutor) Counsel, what is the information on which this question is based?

>   Pros: I had a telephone conversation with
>   Off. Jordan this morning indicating
>   that officers in the Southwest
>   Division had arrested the defendant
>   for battery on a police officer last
>   week.

37. The Court: I'll sustain defense counsel's objection, and direct the jury to draw no inference from the question that Mr. Edwards has been arrested for battery on a police officer.

>   Q: Finally, Mr. Miller, did you know that
>   the defendant was convicted of
>   attempted rape 6 years ago?
>
>   A: No, I did not.
>
>   Pros: Your Honor, in the light of this
>   witness' last answer, the State offers
>   into evidence what has been marked
>   State's Exhibit 4, a certified copy of
>   an Abstract of Judgment, indicating
>   that the defendant Edwards was
>   convicted of attempted rape 6 years
>   ago.

38. The Court: What ruling on the Prosecutor's offer?

>   Q: Nothing further.

Following Miller's testimony, the defense announces its intention to call its last witness, Hy Watermark. By way of an offer of proof, defense counsel states that Mr. Watermark will testify that he is acquainted with Bea Dalton, that he spoke to her about a week after the April 2 attack, and that she mentioned to him that she had had consensual intercourse with Edwards a week before the April 2 attack. The Court has ruled that defense counsel has timely filed the motion and written offer of proof required by FRE 412 (c)(1) and (c)(2). The Court then rules as follows:

39. The Court: Watermark's testimony would be

irrelevant, and he will not be
permitted to testify in this action.

Transcript No. 14: "Character To Impeach" (FRE 608, 609)

A. Background

A party's character is itself rarely an ultimate fact. But the credibility of every witness, be he or she a party to a civil or criminal action, a percipient witness, or an expert, is always in issue. Character evidence is one method of accrediting or attacking a witness' credibility. That is, the credence a trier gives to a witness' testimony may be affected by whether the witness has a propensity to be honest and trustworthy, or the opposite.

The Federal Rules do not allow a party to offer character evidence in support of a witness' credibility until an opposing party has first offered character evidence to attack that same witness' credibility. (FRE 608) For example, assume Party A calls Jenni to testify on direct, "The light was green." Party A cannot offer character evidence in support of Jenni's credibility, as Party B has not yet attacked her character for truthtelling. Assume next that during cross examination of Jenni, Party B elicits evidence that Jenni is biased in favor of Party A. Would this cross entitle Party A to offer evidence that Jenni has a propensity to be honest? No; Party B has attacked Jenni's credibility, but not by means of character evidence. Only after Party B attacks Jenni's credibility with character evidence can Party A offer character evidence to rehabilitate Jenni.

As long as parties maintain this pecking order, the Rules allow them to offer all 3 forms of character evidence: opinion, reputation and specific acts. The latter are generally limited to felonies and lesser crimes involving dishonesty or false statement. (FRE 609 (a)). However, a judge has the discretion to admit evidence of specific acts which did not result in convictions, as long as those acts are probative of truthfulness or untruthfulness. (FRE 608(b)).

In line with the Rules drafters' view that all of us are bundles of independent character traits, character evidence to support or attack credibility is limited to the traits of honesty and trustworthiness, or their opposites. One's everyday inclination to think that a person who is violent may also be untruthful must be set aside in the courtroom. This is a break from the common law tradition, in which any act that might have caused a trier to think ill of a witness was admissible to attack credibility. "How often have you slept with your parrot?" might have been a favorite attack on credibility of common law lawyers. People who still enjoy that sort of inquiry will have to watch daytime television soap operas instead of courtroom trials.

B. <u>Testimony</u>

<u>State v. Relph</u>

Bryan Relph is charged with assault with intent to commit murder. The prosecution contends that Relph slashed Bob Whittington with a knife in a jealous rage, growing out of Relph's delusional belief that Whittington and Relph's wife, Sue, were lovers. Relph contends that he acted in self-defense.

Whittington, the alleged victim of Relph's attack, is called to testify by the prosecution. On direct, Whittington testified that he and Sue Relph were employees in a machine shop. While he did talk with her from time to time, mostly about work-related matters, he never had a social relationship with her, and they certainly had never been intimate. One night Whittington answered a knock on his door and found Relph standing there. At the time, he had no idea of Relph's identity. Relph began yelling angrily about how Whittington was trying to make a fool of him, suddenly began slashing at Whittington with a knife, and fled when Whittington's screams alerted a neighbor. Defense counsel next cross examines Whittington.

<u>Cross Examination of Bob Whittington by Defense Counsel</u>

Q: Mr. Relph appeared on your doorstep one night, is that correct?

A: Yes.

Q: You did not know ahead of time that he might want to see you?

A: Absolutely not.

Q: You know a Trevor Edwards, don't you?

A: Yes, he works at the machine shop.

Q: Isn't it true that about a week before this incident, Mr. Edwards told you that Mr. Relph had told Mr. Edwards that he was very upset because you had been seeing his wife?

D.A: Objection, Your Honor, hearsay.

1. The Court: Overruled.

A: Trevor said something like that.

2. Q: And at the time Mr. Edwards spoke to you, you knew from what Sue Relph had once told you that Mr. Relph had previously beaten up a man in a barroom brawl?

A: I remember she told me that.

Q: So when you saw Mr. Relph standing at your front door on the night of the incident, you had a gun in your hand, didn't you?

D.A: Objection, improper character evidence.

3. The Court: Overruled.

4. A: That's absolutely not true. If Relph says that, he's lying.

5. Q: But you have pointed weapons at other people in the past, haven't you?

116

	A:	Under far different circumstances.
6.	Q:	In fact, you have a lamentable criminal record, don't you?
	A:	I've had a problem or two, but that's all in the past now.
7.	Q:	Well, weren't you recently arrested for indecent exposure?
	A:	I was, but if you check further you'll see that charges were never filed. It was all a big mistake.
8.	Q:	But 3 years ago you were convicted of theft, weren't you?
	A:	That was the only time I've been convicted.
9.	Q:	And that crime involved theft of food from a homeless shelter, didn't it?
	A:	Yes.
	Q:	Weren't you also convicted of perjury last year?
10.	D.A:	Objection, lack of foundation. Counsel, what is the basis for this question?
	Def. Att:	I was informed by counsel in the Public Defender's office that Mr. Whittington had been convicted of perjury.
	D.A:	Renew my objection.
11.	The Court:	What ruling?
	Q:	Finally, Mr. Whittington, I ask you whether at the time of this incident you were addicted to cocaine.
	D.A:	Again, Your Honor, I object as to foundation. I request that counsel state the basis of this question.

> Def. Att: Your Honor, I am simply asking the question. If it is not true, the witness can simply say so.

12. The Court: What ruling?

> Q: Nothing further at this time, Your Honor.

Following Bob Whittington's testimony, the following colloquy took place out of the presence of the jury:

> D.A: Your Honor, defense counsel has attacked the character of Mr. Whittington. Thus, the Government next intends to call Samantha James. By way of an offer of proof, Ms. James will testify that she has been Mr. Whittington's next door neighbor for over 5 years, that she is well acquainted with him, and that in her opinion he is a very trustworthy individual.

> Def. Att: Objection, Your Honor. The defense has not attacked the witness' character for truth-telling by way of reputation or opinion evidence. Thus, Ms. James' testimony would constitute improper rehabilitation.

13. The Court: What ruling?

> D.A: Your Honor, the Government also offers to prove that Ms. James will further testify that last year, she personally observed Mr. Whittington voluntarily enter the local office of the Internal Revenue Service and report that he had discovered an error on his previous year's income tax return which meant he had underreported his tax liability by $2500.

14. Def. Att: You are defense counsel. State what if any objection you would make in response to the Government's second Offer of Proof.

Following the prosecution's resting of its case, the defense made a Motion to Dismiss, which was denied by the trial judge. The defense then opened its case-in-chief and called a witness, Joan Martin, to provide further evidence concerning the character of Bob Whittington.

<u>Direct Examination of Joan Martin by Defense Counsel</u>

15. Q: Ms. Martin, you are a die maker in the machine shop in which Bob Whittington is also employed, is that correct?

    A: Yes.

    Q: How long have you been employed there?

    A: This March will make it 16 years.

    Q: Over what period of time have you known Bob Whittington?

    A: I'd say for about the last 3 years.

    Q: Can you describe the nature of your dealings with him during that time?

    D.A: Objection. Vague and calls for a narrative response.

16. The Court: Sustained.

    Q: Well, would you say that during this 3 year period you've gotten a very good opportunity to become familiar with Whittington's character for telling the truth?

    D. A: Objection, leading and calls for a conclusion.

17. The Court: Sustained.

18. Q: I'll return to this in a moment. First, let me ask you if you recall a conversation you had with Mr. Whittington about six months ago, when

he mentioned a problem he had had in Oklahoma before moving to this state?

A: Yes, we were working an overtime shift, and he started talking about what he called his "days as an Okie."

Q: With specific reference to a problem, what did he tell you?

19. A: He told me that about 6 years earlier, he had served time in Oklahoma for burglary.

Q: Was anyone else present during this conversation?

A: No, just the two of us.

Q: Do you recall where the conversation took place?

A: Well, we were installing a new die for a rush job for a big customer, and we were at that machine.

20. Q: And you're certain that Mr. Whittington told you that he had served time in Oklahoma for burglary?

A: Yes.

Q: Ms. Wilson, over the approximately three year period that you've worked with Mr. Whittington, how often have you seen him?

A: Just about every day, I suppose. Workdays, that is.

Q: Do you ever socialize with him away from the job?

A: Maybe once or twice a month a few of us will have some beers together after work, and sometimes I see him then. Other than that, I just see him around the shop.

21.	Q:	Based on discussions you have had with co-workers, are you aware of Mr. Whittington's reputation for telling the truth?
	A:	Yes.
	Q:	What is that reputation?
22.	A:	He's not considered trustworthy.
	Q:	And based on your own dealings with him, do you have an opinion as to whether Mr. Whittington is trustworthy?
	A:	I do.
	Q:	And what is that opinion?
23.	A:	I do not think he is a very trustworthy person. Even if he's under oath, I wouldn't believe him.
	Q:	Let's be more specific. You heard his testimony earlier in this case, correct?
	A:	Yes, I did.
24.	Q:	If you were the trier of fact, would you believe it?
	A:	No.
	Q:	Can you recall a specific instance in which Mr. Whittington was dishonest?
25.	A:	Just a couple of weeks ago, we had a pile of defective extrusions that the company usually reuses. I saw Whittington collect it and sell it for scrap, and then heard him tell his supervisor that someone had probably broken into the yard overnight and stolen it.
	Q:	Any other instances you can recall?

26. A: I mentioned what I saw to another employee, Sam Thompson, and Sam told me he had seen Whittington do exactly the same thing a month earlier.

   Q: Do you also have an opinion as to whether Mr. Whittington is an aggressive person?

   A: I do.

   Q: And what is that opinion?

27. A: In my opinion, he is a violent and aggressive person.

   Q: Nothing further at this time.

Cross Examination of Joan Wilson by D. A.

28. Q: Ms. Wilson, in the past year you've been sent home from work twice for being intoxicated on the job, isn't that true?

   A: Yes.

   Q: Now, I'd like to call your attention to an incident that occurred last October. Do you recall...

   Def. Att: Excuse me, counsel. Your Honor, may we approach the bench?

   The Court: Well, make it brief.

Proceedings at the Bench

   Def. Att: Your Honor, I believe that the incident that counsel for the Government intends to pursue is improper character evidence, and I wish to make my objection on the record but out of the jury's hearing.

   The Court: Would counsel for the Government make an offer of proof?

   D.A: Certainly. I intend to prove that

last October, the witness and Mr. Whittington mishandled a very large order that cost their employer several thousand dollars. The witness wanted to conceal their mistake from their employer. However, Mr. Whittington refused to do so, and in fact fully disclosed what had happened. As a result, the witness was suspended without pay for 3 weeks and had her car repossessed because she was unable to make payments, but Mr. Whittington was not disciplined.

The Court: And the basis of your objection?

Def. Att: Improper evidence of Ms. Wilson's character, Your Honor.

29. D.A: You are the D.A. What might you say in response to the objection in support of admissibility?

D.A: I also request that in the event that Your Honor rules that the evidence is admissible, but Ms. Wilson denies that the incident occurred, that I be allowed to call Simon Gillig, the supervisor of both Mr. Whittington and Ms. Wilson, to testify that the incident in fact occurred.

Def. Att: In such a case I would object, Your Honor, that Gillig's testimony would be collateral.

30. The Court: What ruling?

Chapter 7

Impeachment

Transcript 15 "Prior Statements" (FRE 801(d)(1))

A. Background

Parties frequently offer evidence of statements made by witnesses prior to the time that the witnesses testify. The Federal Rules admit evidence of such statements pursuant to two general theories. The first allows a party to offer evidence of prior <u>inconsistent</u> statements to <u>impeach</u> (discredit) a witness' testimony. This use of prior inconsistent statements is so well accepted under relevancy principles that no federal rule specifically authorizes it. (FRE 613(b) does, however, prescribe a procedure for offering <u>extrinsic</u> evidence of prior inconsistent statements.)

The second theory under which evidence of prior <u>consistent</u> and <u>inconsistent</u> statements is admissible is for the <u>truth</u> of their contents. In a departure from the common law, the Federal Rules admit prior inconsistent statements for their truth when made under oath during a court proceeding or deposition. Similarly, prior consistent statements are admissible for their truth to rebut a claim that a witness' testimony is a product of a motive to falsify. The fact that the witness made a consistent statement at a time before a motive to falsify existed suggests that the witness' testimony is not a product of the motive. Thus, as when asking for "any sixes" in "Go Fish," the timing of prior consistent statements is everything!

In the same spirit of departure from the common law, the Federal Rules provide that a party can impeach its own witness. (FRE 607) The Rules also jettisoned the "surprise" rule, which provided that a party could not impeach a witness with a prior statement unless the party was "surprised" by the witness' in-court testimony. This change has undoubtedly eliminated Oscar-worthy performances by attorneys who dropped their jaws and clutched their chests in an effort to convince a judge that a witness' testimony had taken them by surprise.

Parties often seek to offer <u>extrinsic</u> evidence of a witness' prior inconsistent statement. Extrinsic evidence refers to a source of a statement other than the witness who made it--e.g., a different witness, or a document. Sometimes a party seeks to offer extrinsic evidence of a prior inconsistent statement after attempting to elicit it on cross examination of a witness who denies making the prior statement. Other times, for tactical reasons, a party prefers to offer extrinsic evidence of a prior inconsistent statement during its own case-in-chief rather than during cross examination of the witness who made the prior statement. The usual tactical reason is that if a party impeaches a witness with a prior inconsistent statement on cross examination, the witness might offer an immediate explanation that negates the impeachment's probative force. By postponing impeachment until offered by an extrinsic source during its own case-in-chief, the impeached witness is unable to immediately explain it away. The procedures set forth in FRE 613 seek to assure that the impeached witness eventually has an opportunity to explain an inconsistency.

However, in neither circumstance is extrinsic evidence of a prior inconsistent statement admissible if the evidence is "collateral." That is, you cannot impeach a witness with extrinsic evidence of a prior inconsistent statement if the information to which the statement pertains is unimportant to the resolution of a dispute. The collateral rule does not forbid cross examination aimed at eliciting a prior inconsistent statement. But if evidence is collateral, you must "take the witness' answer," which means, "no extrinsic evidence."

B. <u>Testimony</u>

<u>In the Matter of Kurt C.</u>

This is a child dependency proceeding in which the State seeks to remove an 8 month old infant, Kurt C., from the custody of his father, Lon Chaney. The State claims that on May 7, Chaney left Kurt alone in a bathtub of scalding hot water.

Summary of Direct Examination of Wes Virginia by Prosecutor

Wes Virginia was called as a witness for the State. On direct examination, Virginia testified that he is a next door neighbor of the Chaney family, which consists of Lon and his son, Kurt. On the afternoon of May 7, walking back home from mailing a package at the post office, Virginia noticed Chaney washing his car in the driveway of Chaney's small bungalow house. Virginia went over to say hello and heard high-pitched cries coming from inside the bungalow. Virginia asked if Kurt was all right; the father replied that there was no problem. Hearing continued cries, Virginia went inside the house and into the bathroom, where he saw Kurt sitting in the bathtub with the water running. The water was scalding; steam was rising from the water in the tub, which was about 15" deep. No other adult was in the house. Virginia removed Kurt from the tub, noticing that his buttocks were red and blistered. He called out to see if anyone else was in the house, and checked all three rooms. When he saw and heard nobody, he took the child outside to Chaney. When Chaney said only, "I'm too busy, you watch him if you're so concerned," Virginia took Kurt into his apartment and called the police.

(The defense evidence will be that Mary O'Bernstein, a teenager who frequently babysat for Kurt, was giving Kurt a bath while Chaney was washing his car. Mary had momentarily gone into Kurt's bedroom to get a towel when Virginia evidently came in and took Kurt. The water in the tub was tepid and Kurt had no injuries when Mary last saw him. Any injuries may have been administered by Virginia, who resented Chaney's raising Kurt with the aid of government assistance.)

Defense counsel now cross examines the neighbor.

Cross Examination of Wes Virginia by Defense Counsel

    Q: Mr. Virginia, isn't it true that you previously told another neighbor of yours, Ethel Mertz, that you had been coming home from collecting your unemployment check when you noticed Mr. Chaney washing his car on May 7?

    Pros: Objection. The prior statement is not under oath, and therefore is inadmissible.

1. The Court: Objection overruled.

    Pros: Also object that counsel is attempting to impeach the witness with a prior statement without having first apprised the witness of the circumstances under which the prior statement was made.

2. The Court: That's not required by the Federal Rules. Objection overruled.

    Pros: Also object that the impeachment is on a collateral matter, as it is unimportant where the witness was coming from before finding the child.

3. The Court: Overruled.

    Pros: Also object that the relevance of the evidence is outweighed by its undue prejudicial effect, as it reveals that the witness is unemployed.

4. The Court: As the issue is one of relevance, under FRE 104(b) I should allow the question as long as there is a sufficient showing to justify a finding that relevance is not outweighed by undue prejudice.

5. The Court: I overrule that objection too.

If the witness can remember what the question was, the witness may answer.

    A: I remember; the answer is no, I didn't say that to Ethel Mertz.

6. Q: You're telling us that your memory is better than Ms. Mertz's?

    A: I just deny saying that.

    Def. Att: Your Honor, I request that the Court permit the defense to call Ms. Mertz during defense case-in-chief to testify that Mr. Virginia did make this statement to her.

7. The Court: What ruling on the request?

    Q: Mr. Virginia, you also had a conversation with Fred Mertz, Ethel's husband, about the events of May 7, isn't that true?

    A: That's possible; I don't remember.

8. Q: Well, would it refresh your recollection if I told you that it was the next morning, May 7, when Mr. Mertz was taking his dog for a walk?

    A: I do remember some discussion with him.

9. Q: And didn't you tell Mr. Mertz that you should have checked to see if anyone else was in the house before taking Kurt out of the tub?

    A: No, I never said anything like that.

    Def. Att: Again, Your Honor, the defense requests permission to call Mr. Mertz as a witness during its case-in-chief to testify that Mr. Virginia did make this statement to him.

10. The Court: What ruling on this request?

Q: In fact, May 7 was a Friday, was it not?

A: I have no idea.

Def. Att: Your Honor, I am handing to the bailiff my "Far Side" calendar for the current year. It indicates that May 7 was a Friday. I ask that the Court examine the calendar and take judicial notice that May 7 was a Friday.

11. The Court: Based on my examination of the calendar, I grant the request.

12. Q: Mr. Virginia, isn't it a fact that on Friday afternoons you often meet some friends at bars for a few drinks?

A: Just once in a while.

Q: Was May 7 a drinking Friday?

A: I'm sure it wasn't.

13. Q: Let's turn to a different topic. According to your statement to the police, the bathtub itself was one of those old-fashioned ones resting on metal legs, correct?

A: Yes, it is.

Q: Do you remember anything unusual about the legs?

A: They were shaped like animal paws, if that's what you mean.

Q: Did you tell the police they were shaped like animal paws?

A: I don't remember.

14. Q: Let the record reflect that I'm showing the witness Exh. 6 for identification, his statement to the police. Mr. Virginia, Exh. 6 does not

say anywhere that the legs were shaped like animal paws, does it?

A: I don't see that in there, no.

Q: Mr. Virginia, were there soap bubbles in the bathtub at the time you say you found Kurt alone in it?

A: I don't remember.

15. Q: Isn't it true that you told Ms. Mertz that you had noticed bubbles in the tub when you found Kurt?

A: If I told her that, then I did.

16. Q: Someone who doesn't care about a baby wouldn't bother to put soap bubbles in the baby's tub, right?

A: Maybe not.

Q: Now, you testified on direct examination that the water in the tub was scalding, correct?

Pros: Objection, asked and answered on direct.

17. The Court: Overruled.

A: Yes, that's right.

Q: But when you spoke to Ms. Mertz, what you said to her is that the water was very hot, correct?

A: I'd say those things mean the same thing.

Q: That's for the trier of fact to determine. I ask that you answer the question.

Pros: I object that this is improper impeachment, as the statement to Ms. Mertz is not inconsistent with the witness' testimony.

18. The Court: I sustain the objection.

    Q: Was water coming out of the bathtub tap when you found Kurt in the tub?

    A: Yes, it was.

    Q: You're sure of that?

    A: Yes.

    Q: Please examine Exh. 6, your statement to the police, once again. It says there, and I quote, "I do not recall whether the water was running when I found Kurt in the tub." Did you make that statement?

    Pros: Objection. In the statement the witness said that he could not recall. Hence, impeachment is improper.

19. The Court: I'll permit the question.

    A: I did. But the next day I noticed that the back of my right hand was all red, and I remembered it was from putting that hand through the running hot water. That's how I now remember that the water was running.

    Def. Att: Move to strike everything after "I did" as non-responsive.

20. The Court: I have no discretion to do so. The witness must be permitted to explain an inconsistency.

    Q: Mr. Virginia, your testimony is that when you entered Mr. Chaney's residence and found the child alone in the tub, you called out to see if anyone else was in the house.

    A: That's right.

    Q: You tried to yell loudly?

    A: Yes. I practically shouted "Anyone here" two or three times.

21. Q: But Ms. O'Bernstein says that she never heard anyone call out, isn't that true?

   A: I know that's what she says.

   Q: Mr. Virginia, how long have you lived in your current residence?

   A: Coming on 6 years now.

   Q: And Mr. Chaney moved in about 5 months before the bathtub incident?

   A: That's about right.

   Q: Shortly after Mr. Chaney moved in, Ms. Mertz told you that he was receiving a family assistance allowance to enable him to afford to rent his house, isn't that true?

   Pros: Objection, hearsay.

   Def. Att: Offered as foundation for the witness' hostility to Mr. Chaney.

22. The Court: For that purpose, overruled.

23. Q: And you replied to Ms. Mertz by saying that welfare cheats like Chaney had no business living in your neighborhood, correct?

   A: I might have said that.

   Q: Didn't you in fact say that to her?

   A: I don't know for sure, I'm just saying that it's possible.

   Def. Att: Your Honor, I'll indicate for the record my intention to call Ms. Mertz during defense case-in-chief to testify that Mr. Virginia did make this statement to her.

   Pros: Objection. The witness has already

conceded that it's possible he did make the statement. Also, it's collateral.

24. The Court: It's not collateral, but the witness has sufficiently answered the question. Let's move on.

Q: Just a couple of more questions. You called the Department of Social Services a week ago, correct?

A: That's right.

Q: You spoke to a Ms. Taten?

A: I think that was her name.

Q: And you asked Ms. Taten if Mr. Chaney would lose his family allowance subsidy if he lost custody of Kurt, correct?

A: I have a right to know that.

Q: And she told you that he would?

A: Yes.

Def. Att: No further questions; after redirect, if any, this witness may be excused. But on direct, Mr. Virginia testified that the water in the tub was 15" deep when he found Kurt. I would indicate to the court that during the defense case-in-chief I intend to call Mr. Mertz to testify that on May 8, the day after the incident, Mr. Virginia told him that the water in the tub was only about 6" deep.

25. The Court: Should the Court permit Mertz to testify to this statement of Mr. Virginia?

The Court: Any redirect?

Pros: A few questions, Your Honor.

Redirect Examination of Wes Virginia by Prosecutor

26. Q: Just so we're clear, you saw or heard no one else in the house at the time you saw Kurt in the bathtub?

    A: That's right.

    Q: You testified on direct that you are a graphics designer on temporary furlough from your company. About how many employees work for that company?

    A: Usually about 35-40 employees.

    Q: How long have you been employed there?

    A: For over 14 years.

    Q: Do you have a reputation as far as truth and honesty goes among your co-workers?

    A: Yes, I do.

    Q: And what is that reputation?

    Def. Att: Objection, improper character evidence.

    Pros: Counsel attempted on cross to discredit Mr. Virginia. This is proper rehabilitation.

27. The Court: Objection overruled.

    A: I have an excellent reputation for telling the truth.

    Q: One last area. Do you know a woman by the name of Enid Okla?

    A: Yes, we've been neighbors for years.

    Q: Do you recall discussing this case with her?

    A: Yes, about a month ago, I'd say.

Q: Did you discuss whether anyone was in the house at the time you found Kurt in the tub?

A: We did talk about that.

Q: What did you tell her?

Def. Att: Objection, hearsay.

Pros: Offered as a prior consistent statement under FRE 801(d)(1)(B) to show that Mr. Virginia's testimony is not a product of his conversation with Ms. Taten.

The Court: Both counsel approach the bench so that the prosecutor can make an offer of proof.

Pros (At the bench): The witness will testify that he told Ms. Okla that he still had trouble sleeping at night because of finding a baby all alone in a house in a bathtub.

28. The Court: What ruling?

Transcript 16: "Contradiction, Bias and Other Methods of Attacking Credibility"

A. Background

General relevance principles (FRE 401) make evidence pertaining to the credibility of witnesses admissible unless the evidence conflicts with a specific (e.g., inadmissible character evidence) or general (e.g., FRE 403) exclusionary rule. Hence, evidence tending to prove that a witness' testimony is mistaken, a product of bias or interest, or for some other reason of dubious credibility is routinely offered and admitted.

An oft-intoned evidentiary principle suggests that evidence <u>accrediting</u> a witness is not admissible until after the witness' credibility has been attacked. The assertion is not totally without foundation. For example, FRE 801 (d)(1)(B) bars evidence of prior consistent statements until after evidence tending to prove that testimony is a product of recent fabrication or improper motive has been offered. Often, however, you can offer accrediting evidence without regard to whether a witness' credibility has been attacked. For instance, assume that during initial direct examination, an eyewitness identifies the defendant as the person who committed a crime. Even before cross examination, you can offer evidence bolstering the credibility of the identification, such as the excellent lighting at the scene of the crime and the witness' close proximity to the defendant. Similarly, you might elicit testimony that the witness has never seen the defendant previously, and thus has no axe to grind.

Extrinsic impeachment evidence is not admissible if the evidence is collateral. Evidence suggesting bias or interest is traditionally regarded as non-collateral. Contradiction evidence, by contrast, may be collateral. Thus, extrinsic evidence is not admissible to contradict a witness' testimony unless the testimony pertains to a significant item of proof.

B. <u>Testimony</u>

<u>Hawthorne v. Telstar Pictures Corp.</u>

Plaintiff Edgar Allen Hawthorne has sued Telstar claiming that Telstar wrongfully appropriated his story idea in producing the hit motion picture, <u>Littler Women</u>. The defendant concedes that a number of similarities between Hawthorne's story idea and the motion picture exist, but denies that it knew in advance of making the picture of Hawthorne or of his story, and denies that the picture was based in any way on Hawthorne's material.

One of Hawthorne's witnesses is Bea Sharpe. On direct examination, Sharpe testified that preceding the release of <u>Littler Women</u>, she was working as a reader at Telstar. As a reader, her duties included reviewing manuscripts and making recommendations as to their likely commercial success as motion pictures. Sometimes her boss, Fay Dout, would assign manuscripts for Sharpe to review; other times, Sharpe would on her own select one from "The Pile," which consisted of unsolicited manuscripts. One of the manuscripts Sharpe found in The Pile was Hawthorne's story treatment, then titled <u>People With Some Personal Problems</u>. She thought it had excellent potential, and in July, along with a cover memo summarizing the story, forwarded the manuscript to Dout for further review. This occurred about three months before the circulation of a Telstar memo describing projects the company was working on. One of the projects mentioned in the memo was <u>Littler Women</u>; the screenplay was attributed to Fay Dout and another writer, Linda Marrow. Sharpe spoke to Dout about the similarity between <u>Littler Women</u> and the Hawthorne materials, but Dout told her she knew nothing about the Hawthorne materials, and asked Sharpe never to mention the subject again.

Telstar's counsel now cross examines Sharpe.

<u>Cross Examination of Bea Sharpe by Defense Counsel</u>

Q: Ms. Sharpe, you found the Hawthorne story treatment in a group of manuscripts called The Pile?

A: That's correct.

Q: At the time you read the Hawthorne manuscript, you had been employed as a reader for over five years, correct?

A: Yes, about three years with Telstar, and before that I was at Megatrend.

1. Q: You never were promoted to a higher position by Telstar, were you?

A No, but I got cost-of-living increases.

Q: Now, Megatrend also maintained an area similar to The Pile for unsolicited manuscripts, correct?

A: Yes, I think all producers do.

2. Q: Based on your experience, wouldn't you agree that it is unusual for a manuscript from The Pile to be produced as a motion picture?

A: I suppose that's right.

Q: That's right. And isn't it also right that Hawthorne lied to get his manuscript even onto The Pile by telling a Telstar receptionist that he had once had a play of his produced?

Pl. Att: I ask that the Court admonish counsel not to repeat the witness' answer before asking a question.

3. The Court: Yes, counsel, please refrain from that. If it happens again, I'll hold you in contempt of court.

Pl. Att: Object also that it is irrelevant how Mr. Hawthorne's manuscript found its way into The Pile.

4. The Court: Well, it goes to the plaintiff's character for telling the truth. I'll permit it.

   Pl. Att: Also object, lack of foundation.

5. The Court: Sustained.

   Q: Ms. Sharpe, do you recall attending a premiere of <u>The Dirtier Dozen</u> with your brother, Luke?

   A: Yes.

   Q: Didn't you say to him at that premiere that most current productions were nothing more than "B" grade exploitation movies?

   Pl. Att: Objection, hearsay and irrelevant.

   Def. Att: It's not hearsay, as it goes to the witness' bias against Telstar as a movie producer.

6. The Court: For that purpose, it's not hearsay. But I sustain the objection on relevance grounds.

7. Q: Let's move on. Isn't it true that Telstar promised each reader whose review of a manuscript from The Pile resulted in a finished movie a bonus of $5000?

   A: Yes.

   Q: In fact you've instituted your own suit against Telstar for that amount?

   Pl. Att: Objection, counsel is attacking the witness' right of access to the courts.

8. The Court: Overruled.

   A: I have, yes.

> Q: And aren't both you and Mr. Hawthorne elders in the local Church of the Divine Experience?
>
> Pl. Att: Objection. Under FRE 610, counsel cannot question the witness about her religious beliefs.

9. The Court: Overruled. Witness may answer.

> A: We are. But the Church teaches to tell the truth at all times.
>
> Def. Att: Move to strike the last sentence, and ask the jury to disregard it.

10. The Court: What ruling?

> Q: How did you happen to locate the Hawthorne manuscript in The Pile?
>
> A: I was going on holiday to the Costa Brava area of Spain for a week in July, so I decided to bring along a few manuscripts from The Pile with me. I quickly leafed through about 15 manuscripts, and Hawthorne's was one of the five I brought on my holiday.
>
> Q: How many manuscripts were in The Pile at the time?
>
> A: I'm not really sure; quite a few.
>
> Q: What is quite a few? 30? 50? 100?
>
> A: I can't tell you precisely, probably somewhere between 50 and 75.
>
> Q: Was it closer to 50 or to 75?
>
> Pl. Att: Objection, argumentative. The witness has given her best estimate.
>
> Def. Att: I'm entitled to test the witness' recollection.

11. The Court: You've gotten a sufficient answer. Move on.

12. Q: You testified that you looked through about 15 manuscripts. In your deposition you stated that you could not recall any of their titles except Hawthorne's, correct?

    A: That's right.

    Q: When did you submit the Hawthorne manuscript and your review to Ms. Dout?

    A: My first day back from vacation. I was really excited about it.

    Q: Ms. Dout was your supervisor, correct?

    A: She was.

    Q: Before she was made supervisor, you had applied for the position?

    A: Yes I had.

13. Q: You resent Telstar management for giving her the job instead of you, don't you?

    A: Well, I was disappointed of course. But I wouldn't say I was resentful.

14. Q: And after Hawthorne filed suit, you wrote a letter to the Telstar Board of Directors accusing Ms. Dout of plagiarism, correct?

    A: I sure did.

    Q: And you mailed a copy to the local paper?

    Pl. Att: Objection, cumulative.

15. The Court: I'll permit it.

    A: Yes.

    Q: Telstar fired you the day after the letter was published?

A: Yes.

16. Q: Around the time that you say you were reading the Hawthorne manuscript, you were a habitual user of alcohol, correct?

A: I had a little drinking problem, yes.

17. Q: And on at least two occasions during the week holiday when you say you read the Hawthorne manuscript, you ingested cocaine?

A: No I did not.

Def. Att: Nothing further at this time.

After the plaintiff rested his case, defendant made a motion to dismiss, which was denied. The defense now presents its case-in-chief; the first witness is Lars Josefson.

Direct Examination of Lars Josefson by Defense Counsel

Q: Mr. Josefson, you worked with Bea Sharpe at Megatrend and remain friendly with her, correct?

Pl. Att: Objection, leading.

18. The Court: Overruled.

A: Yes, that's right.

Q: Do you know the circumstances under which her employment with Megatrend terminated?

19. A: Yes. Megatrend has a drug testing program, and she told me that she twice failed drug tests.

Q: Did you hear Ms. Sharpe testify that she forwarded the Hawthorne manuscript along with her positive recommendation to Fay Dout in July of last year?

A: I did.

20. Q: Would you describe yourself as a good friend of Ms. Sharpe?

    A: Yes, I'd say so. We meet for lunch every couple of weeks, and talk on the phone pretty regularly.

    Q: Would you discuss manuscripts you were working on?

    A: Well, not too much. After all, we were working for competitors.

    Q: Mr. Josefson, isn't it a fact that while she was working at Telstar, Ms. Sharpe frequently told you about manuscripts that she was reading?

    Pl. Att: Objection, leading. Also, defense is attempting to impeach its own witness.

21. The Court: Overruled.

    A: I guess you could say so.

    Q: Did she at any time mention the Hawthorne manuscript to you?

    A: No.

    Pl. Att: Objection, improper impeachment. Counsel excused Ms. Sharpe without questioning her about a conversation she may have had with Mr. Josefson about the Hawthorne manuscript, and thus under FRE 613 counsel is foreclosed from asking this witness about it.

22. The Court: No, I'll permit it.

    Pl. Att: Object also that it's irrelevant. Ms. Sharpe may have had many reasons for not telling this witness about the Hawthorne manuscript, including the fact he works for a competitor.

    Def. Att: In light of the witness'

testimony that Sharpe spoke to him about manuscripts she was working on, the jury may infer that her failure to mention the Hawthorne manuscript supports our theory that she never saw it.

23. The Court: I should sustain the objection unless I find that the relevant inference is stronger than the irrelevant ones.

24. The Court: I'll sustain that objection and strike the answer.

Q: Mr. Josefson, did you see Ms. Sharpe while she was on holiday in July of last year?

A: I did, quite by accident really. It turned out that I was sent over on business to the same area where she was on vacation. She was there for a week, I was there a few days longer.

Q: Which area was it where you saw her on holiday in July?

A: She was in Keswick, in the Lake District of England.

Pl. Att: Objection and move to strike, irrelevant.

Def. Att: Admissible to impeach Ms. Sharpe's testimony that she was on holiday on the Costa Brava in Spain. An inaccuracy about that might well cause the jury to disbelieve her other testimony.

25. The Court: Objection sustained. The answer will be stricken.

Q: Do you know whether she was reading manuscripts while on holiday?

26. A: A couple of times I saw her reading

what looked like unsolicited manuscripts, and when I asked her she told me that is what they were.

Q: Did you ask her how many manuscripts she had taken with her on holiday?

A: Yes, and she said she remembered at the last minute that she wanted to bring some manuscripts to read, so she just ran over to "The Pile" and grabbed four or five manuscripts off the top.

Pl. Att: Objection and move to strike, this is a prior inconsistent statement offered on a collateral matter.

27. The Court: What ruling?

Q: Mr. Josefson, do you know whether Ms. Sharpe is personally acquainted with the plaintiff, Hawthorne?

28. A: My wife and I have accompanied them on a number of dates, yes.

Q: And has Ms. Sharpe ever spoken to you about Hawthorne?

A: She has told me more than once that Hawthorne is a great writer who has a brilliant future in movies.

Pl. Att: Objection and move to strike, hearsay.

29. Def. Att: Assume that you are defense counsel. What response would you make to the objection?

Q: Finally, are you acquainted with Fay Dout?

A: Oh, yes. We're both active in many industry activities; I know her quite well.

Q: Do you have an opinion as to her personal integrity?

30. A: Yes, I have the highest regard for her personal integrity.

Q: Nothing further at this time.

The Court: Cross examination?

Cross Examination of Lars Josefson by Plaintiff's Counsel

31. Q: Mr. Josefson, you've applied for employment as a reader at Telstar, isn't that correct?

    A: I have; is there a problem with that?

    Pl. Att: I think there's a problem, the problem being that you may well be slanting your testimony in an effort to curry favor at Telstar.

    Def. Att: Object to counsel making statements instead of asking questions.

    Pl. Att: The witness asked me a question, I'm entitled to answer it.

32. The Court: I'll strike the remark and admonish the jury to disregard it. Plaintiff's counsel is to refrain from further comments on the evidence.

33. Q: Last year, Mr. Josefson, you were convicted of misdemeanor assault, were you not?

    A: That's true.

34. Q: As a professional reader, you yourself have never had an unsolicited manuscript which you have reviewed on your own initiative made into a movie, correct?

    A: That's true.

    Q: Mr. Josefson, within a few days after you returned from your business trip you spoke to Ms. Sharpe, correct?

A: I'm sure I did. As I said, we spoke to each other pretty regularly.

Q: In particular, she called you at your office in early August?

A: I think she did.

Q: Didn't she tell you at that time that she had read an unsolicited manuscript on her trip that she thought would make a great movie?

A: No, I don't remember her saying that.

Pl. Att: For the record, Your Honor, plaintiff intends to call a rebuttal witness, Marc Sucherman, a colleague of Josefson's at Megatrend, to testify that after Josefson finished speaking to Ms. Sharpe in early August, Josefson told Sucherman that Ms. Sharpe had said that she had read an unsolicited manuscript on her holiday that she thought would make a great movie.

35. The Court: Should Sucherman be permitted to testify?

Chapter 8

Examining Forgetful Witnesses

Transcript 17 (FRE 607, 611 (c), 612, 803 (5))

A. <u>Background</u>

Witnesses often fail to recall information that they have either testified to during a pre-trial deposition, or described during an informal interview. Forgetfulness may be a product of the direct examiner confusing a witness by eliciting information in an unexpected order, or of opposing counsel interrupting testimony with numerous objections. Or, it may simply be a product of the stress of testifying in a formal atmosphere.

Whatever the cause of forgetfulness, the rules of evidence do not bind attorneys to a witness' initial response. Through the rubrics of refreshing recollection, offering "past recollection recorded," and impeaching one's own witness, attorneys can "correct" a witness' incomplete or erroneous response. This seems sensible: since evidentiary rules place few limits on attorneys' discussions with potential witnesses in the privacy of the attorneys' offices, a flexible approach is warranted when an attorney seeks to have a witness amend testimony in open court. (Of course, what rules of evidence allow, principles of persuasion may take away. Evidence may be less credible when it has to be extracted like an impacted wisdom tooth from a forgetful witness.)

Evidentiary rules are most flexible when a questioner seeks to jog a witness' present recollection. Leading questions are permissible under FRE 611 (c), and FRE 612 provides for the use of writings of nearly any ilk to revive a witness' recollection. But FRE 803 (5) imposes stricter foundational requirements when a witness' previous statements are offered in lieu of the witness' present recollection.

B. <u>Testimony</u>

O'Hare v. Hutchinson
(Same case as in Transcript 4)

Civil suit for damages for personal injuries suffered by O'Hare as a result of having been struck on September 22 by a car driven by Hutchinson. O'Hare claims that he was in a crosswalk at the intersection of Main and Peach Streets when Hutchinson negligently made a left turn into Main, striking and injuring O'Hare. Testifying on behalf of O'Hare is Marcia Diedrich, who has thus far testified that just prior to the collision, she was stopped on Main waiting for the light to change to green. She saw O'Hare step into the crosswalk to cross Main Street, then noticed Hutchinson traveling along Peach at 30-35 m.p.h. and fail to slow down as she made a left turn onto Main. Diedrich has further testified that though she did not see Hutchinson's car strike O'Hare, no more than a few seconds elapsed between the time she saw O'Hare in the crosswalk and the time that Hutchinson struck O'Hare. Hutchinson contends that she was driving carefully, and that O'Hare was struck not in the crosswalk, but about 25 yards up the block when he suddenly ran out from between two parked cars. The direct of Diedrich continues; the direct examiner primarily seeks to have the witness testify to a statement Hutchinson made just after striking O'Hare.

Direct Examination of Diedrich by Plaintiff's Attorney

Q: Ms. Diedrich, after you heard the impact, what happened next?

A: I looked over and saw Mr. O'Hare lying on the street in front of Ms. Hutchinson's truck. Then I saw her jump out of the truck and go to check on Mr. Hutchinson.

Q: How far was Mr. O'Hare lying from where Ms. Hutchinson's truck had come to a stop?

A: I'd say just a couple of feet.

1. Q: Could it have been more like 10 feet?

   A: That's possible.

2. Q: Well, haven't you previously given me a written statement in which you say that the distance was 10 feet?

   A: Oh, yes, that's right. Sorry, I was confused.

   Q: All right, Ms. Diedrich, after the defendant went over to check on Ms. O'Hare what happened?

3. A: She stood over him just for a couple of seconds, then ran into a nearby store to call for an ambulance.

   Q: Before she ran into the store, did she say anything to Mr. O'Hare?

   A: I don't remember anything.

4. Q: Did she say anything about the crosswalk?

   A: I just can't remember.

5. Q: Please think hard. Try to recall whether Ms. Hutchinson said something about not seeing Mr. O'Hare in the crosswalk.

   A: I'm sorry, my mind's a blank.

   Pl. Att: Your Honor, I have the Police Report relating to this incident prepared by Off. Spajik and dated September 22. Defense counsel has a copy. May it be marked Plaintiff's 1 for identification?

   Def. Att: Objection that the report is hearsay.

6. The Court: At this time counsel is simply marking the report as an exhibit; I'll permit that.

Q: Ms. Diedrich, please examine the report, and in particular the portion on page 2 that I've underlined, and see if that refreshes your recollection as to whether Ms. Hutchinson made a statement to Mr. O'Hare.

Def. Att: Your Honor, the report was prepared by Off. Spajik, not this witness. I object to its being shown.

7. The Court: I'll overrule that objection.

Q: Have you had an opportunity to examine the report?

A: Yes.

8. Q: And can you now remember whether Ms. Hutchinson made a statement to Mr. O'Hare?

A: Well, I see here that Ms. Hutchinson said that she never saw Mr. O'Hare in the crosswalk.

Def. Att: Objection and move to strike, hearsay.

9. The Court: Sustained. The answer will be stricken, and the jury is instructed to disregard it.

Q: Ms. Hutchinson, without reference to what might be stated in the report, can you now remember whether Ms. Hutchinson made a statement to Ms. O'Hare?

A: No, I remember she said something, and I remember it was "Oh my God" something, but beyond that I really don't remember what she said.

Pl. Att: Your Honor, for the court's information, I will endeavor to lay a foundation qualifying the statement as the witness' past recollection recorded.

10. The Court: You may proceed, counsel. For the record once you lay a <u>prime facie</u> foundation, defense counsel has the burden, by a preponderance of the evidence, of showing that the foundation is not adequate.

Q: Let me ask you this, Ms. Diedrich. Do you remember Ms. Hutchinson making a statement to Mr. O'Hare?

A: Yes, I do remember that.

Q: And did you tell Off. Spajik what Ms. Hutchinson had said?

A: Yes.

Q: When did you tell Off. Spajik what you had heard Ms. Hutchinson say?

A: I guess it was about an hour and a half later.

Q: Was there any reason for your taking that long?

A: I was pretty shook up by what happened, and I noticed other people stopping to help. I was on my way to an appointment, so I just went there. Then I drove back to Peach and Main, and saw that an officer was still there, so I told him what I knew.

11. Q: Were you able to accurately tell the officer what had happened?

A: Yes, things were still fresh in my memory.

Pl. Att: Your Honor, I have a request that's a little unusual, but I understand that we may be featured in an evidence book. To make the book read more smoothly, might I momentarily interrupt the testimony of this witness to call Off. Spajik to the stand for further foundational testimony?

The Court: You may.

Direct Examination of Off. Spajik by Attorney for Plaintiff

(preliminary questions omitted)

Q: Off. Spajik, do you recall talking to Marcia Diedrich, the lady who was just testifying, at the scene of the accident?

A: Yes. I had nearly concluded my investigation when she came up to me.

Q: And did she make a statement to you?

A: A brief one, yes sir.

Q: Did you record that statement accurately?

A: Yes.

Pl. Att: At this time, Your Honor, I would ask that the portion of Off. Spajik's report that I have underlined, the statement by Ms. Diedrich, be received in evidence.

Def. Att: I have a few questions by way of voir dire for Ms. Diedrich, Your Honor.

Voir Dire Examination of Marcia Diedrich by Defense Counsel

12. Q: Ms. Diedrich, your testimony that Ms. Hutchinson was going 30-35 m.p.h. on Peach as she made her left turn onto Main is simply an estimate, isn't that right?

    A: I suppose that's true.

    Q: Now, you testified you were on your way to an appointment. What sort of appointment was it?

A: I was meeting with a teacher at my child's school.

Q: And did you discuss the accident you had just witnessed part of with the teacher?

A: Yes. In fact, he told me about a very similar one he had seen about 6 months earlier.

Q: Please tell us what you can remember that the teacher told you.

Pl. Att: Objection, beyond the scope of direct. I asked nothing about a different accident, or what she and the teacher talked about. Also, what the teacher told her is objected to as hearsay.

13. The Court: Both objections are overruled. The witness may answer.

A: He told me he had been walking when he saw a car run a red light and hit a pedestrian who was just starting to cross a street in a crosswalk.

Q: Did the teacher hear the driver of the car that ran the light make a statement of any kind?

A: He said he had talked to the driver afterward, and that the driver had said something about not being able to see the light or the pedestrian because the sun was directly in his eyes.

Q: Ms. Diedrich, before you were called to testify here, did Mr. O'Hare's counsel give you any documents to review to help you prepare?

A: I remember he gave me a copy of my deposition, a written statement that counsel had asked Mr. O'Hare to prepare, and a written statement prepared for O'Hare's counsel by some other witness I've never met.

Def. Att: Your Honor, I have a copy of Ms. Diedrich's deposition, but I request that plaintiff's counsel furnish me at this time with a copy of the written statements to which the witness has just referred.

14. The Court: What ruling?

Q: One last question. When you returned to Peach and Main, did you speak with Mr. O'Hare before you spoke with Off. Spajik?

Pl. Att: Objection, irrelevant.

Def. Att: Might I be heard? The relevance is that if the witness did speak to Mr. O'Hare, it shows a further lack of freshness, and affects the witness' credibility.

15. The Court: The objection will be overruled.

The Court: Anything further from the plaintiff?

Direct Examination of Diedrich by Plaintiff's Attorney

16. Q: Ms. Diedrich, did you mention to the teacher what Hutchinson had said following the accident before or after the teacher told you about the accident he had seen?

A: I don't recall.

Pl. Att: At this time, I offer the portion of the police report containing the statement made by Ms. Diedrich to Off. Spajik concerning what she heard Mr. Hutchinson say into evidence as the witness' past recollection recorded.

Def. Att: Objection, hearsay.

17. The Court: Overruled.

   Def. Att: I also object that the statement does not qualify as past recollection recorded. The time delay of one and a half hours, combined with the witness' speaking both to her child's teacher about a similar accident and to Mr. O'Hare, indicates that the matter was not fresh in the witness' memory when she spoke to the officer.

18. The Court: I'll overrule that objection.

   Def. Att: I also object to receipt of the police report, or any portion of it, into evidence.

19. The Court: Overruled.

Chapter 9

Expert Testimony

Transcript 18 (FRE 702, 703, 704, 705)

A. Background

Expert testimony is permissible when a trier's judgment about the relevance or probative value of evidence might be aided by a person with specialized knowledge and/or experience. For example, assume that in a prosecution for felony drunk driving, a witness were to testify that one hour before the defendant got behind the wheel, the defendant was in a cocktail lounge and had consumed four Manhattans. Expert testimony that the defendant was probably under the influence of alcohol when driving would probably not be permissible. The opinion of an expert would not be of aid to the trier of fact, whose common knowledge and experience would be more than adequate to infer from the evidence that the defendant was under the influence of alcohol while driving.

By contrast, assume that a wearer of contact lenses sues a contact lens manufacturer for manufacturing a set of defective lenses. The plaintiff claims to have suffered a detached cornea as a result of wearing the allegedly defective lenses. In such a case, a lay trier of fact would not have sufficient experience to examine the plaintiff's eye and determine that the cornea is detached, or to determine whether the contact lens was defective, or to determine whether a defect in the contact lens was the cause of the detached cornea. An expert, undoubtedly an ophthalmologist of some sort, would have to point out to the trier the relevant evidence ("What you're looking at here is a scratched cornea"), and provide specialized knowledge enabling the trier to draw an inference ("The interior surface of a contact lens would not be this rough unless it were defective."). Doing away with decades of hair-splitting, FRE 704 would even permit an expert to tell a trier directly what inference to draw

("My opinion is that this contact lens was manufactured defectively.").

As a reward to experts for pleasing their parents by acquiring expertise, when experts do testify the Federal Rules relax many of the evidentiary principles that constrict the testimony of lay witnesses:

1. Experts need not have personally observed the events about which they testify. (FRE 703)

2. Experts can base their opinions on hearsay as well as other forms of inadmissible evidence, as long as the evidence is of the sort that experts of that ilk usually rely on. (FRE 703) Of course, no matter what the practice among experts, expert witnesses cannot rely on evidence whose use would violate important policies. For example, an accident reconstruction expert usually cannot base an opinion, even in part, on the inadmissible hearsay statements of bystanders or on a confession wrung out of a driver by repeated playing of the last act of "Tosca."

3. Unlike lay witnesses (see FRE 602), experts can testify to their opinions without first disclosing the data on which those opinions are based. (FRE 705)

4. Experts are entitled to be paid for their testimony.

5. Finally, some experts get to wear white coats and stethoscopes when they testify.

6. However, the Federal Rules are not without their bite: on cross examination, an expert can be confronted with statements in published authorities established as reliable. (FRE 803(18)).

Some of the most controversial evidentiary issues involve the admissibility of novel forms of expert testimony, notably scientific evidence such as DNA testing. Debate centers both on the validity of the scientific method, and on the standard by which the court is to evaluate validity. As to the latter, the most common test remains the "Frye" test, under which a court does not admit novel scientific evidence until the technique through which the evidence was produced has been generally accepted by the relevant scientific community. However, many courts today regard the "Frye" test as unduly conservative, and opt to evaluate the validity of novel scientific methods under general relevancy principles.

Expert testimony is not limited to scientific evidence. Any area of specialized knowledge may, if relevant, be the basis of expert testimony. For example, a plumber may be sufficiently qualified to render an expert opinion as to what caused a pipe to burst. Therefore, the foundation for expert testimony may consist of a person's <u>formal education and training</u>: undergraduate and postgraduate degrees, specific courses taken, "continuing education" courses. It may consist of a person's <u>special knowledge and skills</u>: licenses; specialty certifications; professional associations; courses taught; books or articles written; previous testimony as an expert. Or, it may consist only of a person's <u>special experience</u>: occupation; job duties.

Attorneys often offer to bypass the foundation necessary to qualify a witness as an expert by stipulating to an expert's qualifications. The party calling the expert may not want to accept the stipulation, on the ground that the magnificence of a particular expert's background is relevant not only to foundation but also to credibility: "The jury should hear that this person has won 3 Nobel prizes and earned 37 Cub Scout Merit Badges." A court's decision to enforce a foundational stipulation relating to expertise on an unwilling party is generally committed to the court's sound discretion.

B. <u>Testimony</u>

<u>Wood B. Widower v. Atlas Insurance Co.</u>

Plaintiff Widower has brought suit against Atlas seeking to recover the proceeds of a life insurance policy on the life of his wide, Wilma, of which he is the beneficiary. Widower's claim is based on testimony that neither he nor anyone else with whom Wilma could be expected to be in contact has seen or heard from her since she left the family home to buy groceries over seven years ago. In Widower's jurisdiction, the evidence is sufficient to give rise to a rebuttable presumption that Wilma is deceased.

The insurance company now offers evidence in support of its contention that Wilma is still alive and that it therefore is not obligated to pay the proceeds of the policy to the plaintiff. The evidence concerns a message that was left on Widower's phone answering machine about three months before the suit was filed. The company claims that the voice is that of Widower's wife Wilma, and calls as a witness Dr. Ian Peters in support of that claim. Dr. Peters is a Professor of Linguistics and an expert in "voiceprint" analysis. This is a technique of identifying voices by comparing a sample of a "known" voice with that of an "unknown" voice. The comparison is aided by a device known as a "spectrograph," which produces a graphic representation (a "spectrogram") of various qualities of the human voice. In this case, Dr. Peters prepared spectrograms of the message on Widower's phone answering machine (the unknown voice) and of a taped message made about nine years earlier and conceded to be the voice of Wilma (the known voice). After listening to both tapes and comparing the spectrograms, Dr. Peters concluded that both voices belonged to the same person, Wilma. If believed, Dr. Peters' testimony rebuts the presumption that Wilma is deceased and would produce a judgment that Atlas is not required to pay the proceeds of the policy to the plaintiff.

The plaintiff's theory is that Dr. Peter's analysis was flawed and his opinion inaccurate. His counsel intends to raise serious doubts about the doctor's opinion on cross and will not call an opposing linguistics expert.

Note: As you analyze the transcript below, assume that your jurisdiction has, in accord with a number of others, decided that testimony based on voice spectrographic analysis is admissible. Thus, a foundation establishing the scientific community's acceptance of the technique is unnecessary.

<u>Direct Examination of Dr. Ian Peters by Defense Counsel</u>

Q: Dr. Peters, what is your current position?

A: I am Professor of Linguistics at NYUCLA.

Q: Please tell us what degrees you've received.

Pl. Att: Objection, calls for a narrative.

1. The Court: Overruled.

A: I hold a B.A. and an M.A. from Oxford, both in English Languages. I received the former 26 years ago, the latter four years later. Thirteen years ago, I received a Ph.D in Linguistics from NYUCLA.

Q: Do you have a particular area of expertise within the field of linguistics?

A: Linguistics itself is the study of different languages. My specialty is phonetics, the study of speech sounds.

Q: Did you do any teaching before coming to NYUCLA?

A: Yes. Between the time I received my B.A. and my M.A., I taught English and French at Prempeh College in Ghana. After I received my Masters, I was a Lecturer for four years in the Department of Linguistics at the University of Jos in Nigeria. I have been at NYUCLA since receiving my doctorate, advancing seven years ago to the position of full professor.

Q: Dr. Peters, are you a member of any professional societies?

A: Yes indeed. I belong to the Acoustical Society of America, the Linguistic Society of America, the International Phonetic Association, and the West African Linguistic Society.

Pl. Att: Your Honor, to save time we'll stipulate that Dr. Peters is an expert in spectrographic analysis.

Def. Att: I'd ask to be allowed to establish the foundation for this witness' expertise. The area of expertise is one with which the jurors are unfamiliar, and the foundation will better enable them to understand the witness' testimony.

2. The Court: I'll permit counsel to elicit additional foundational testimony, subject to further objection by the plaintiff should the foundational questioning become overly extended.

Q: Approximately how many articles concerning the identification of speakers though speech sounds have you published?

Pl. Att: Objection, leading and assumes facts not in evidence.

3. The Court: Overruled.

A: I'd estimate about 20.

Q: Could you please give us some idea of what these publications are about?

Pl. Att: Objection, irrelevant. Also, relevance is outweighed by undue consumption of time. Also object as vague.

4. The Court: The objection is sustained on the latter two grounds.

5. Q: Specifically, have you published any books or articles concerning the use of voiceprints to identify speakers?

   A: No, I haven't. Actually, I personally do not use the term "voiceprint." It implies that people's vocal qualities do not change from one moment to the next, but of course we know that they do. If someone whispers on one occasion and yells on another, certainly the spectrograms will differ.

   Q: Are you familiar with the device known as a sound spectrograph?

   A: Rather; I use it constantly in my research and teaching.

   Q: Can you please describe its operation for us?

   Pl. Att: Objection, overly broad.

6. The Court: Overruled.

   A: Essentially, it is a machine that enables a short portion of speech, between two to three seconds, to be recorded onto a loop. The loops are passed through a series of filters that separate the sounds into the three characteristics of speech sounds: time duration; frequency, which you might also refer to as pitch; and loudness. The machine produces a graph, known as a spectrogram, depicting each aspect of speech. Time is shown along the horizontal leg of the graph from left to right, frequency along the vertical axis, and loudness is represented by the darkness of the speech pattern.

   Q: How do you use spectrograms in your work?

A: In a variety of ways. Sometimes I use them to examine ethnic differences in speech sounds. Of more relevance here, I often use them to determine if different speech samples were produced by the same speaker.

7. Q: In order to determine if two different spectrograms are from the same speaker, I take it that you have to you compare the graphs for the same speech sound?

A: Yes, though more precisely I'd want to have the same speech sound in the same word. For example, I'd want to find the vowel sound "e" in the same word, such as "green," in both spectrograms, rather than finding it in the word "green" in one spectrogram and in the word "see" in the other.

8. Q: Have you previously qualified to testify as an expert in spectrographic analysis?

A: Yes, five times I believe. I have also been consulted numerous times in cases in which I would have testified, but they were resolved before trial.

Q: Dr. Peters, were you asked to identify two samples of recorded speech which allegedly were made by Wilma Widower?

Pl. Att: Your Honor, it appears that counsel intends to get into the substance of this witness' testimony. Despite my previous offer to stipulate to the witness' qualifications, I ask to be permitted to take the witness on voir dire for the purpose of exploring the adequacy of the foundation.

9. The Court: Well, it's a little irregular to engage in voir dire after you've offered to stipulate, but this is after all a teaching book where things like this might happen. I'll permit you to question the witness now rather

than waiting until cross examination, but only as to matters going to the witness' qualifications.

10. The Court: I will have the jurors remain present during the voir dire examination, as a ruling that the witness is qualified to give expert testimony is preliminary; the jurors make the final decision as to whether the witness is qualified to give expert testimony if and when the case is submitted to them.

<u>Voir Dire Examination of Dr. Ian Peters by Plaintiff's Counsel</u>

Q: Dr. Peters, you've never published anything about using spectrographic analysis to identify a speaker?

Def. Att: Objection, asked and answered.

11. The Court: Overruled.

A: That's true.

12. Q: Each of the four linguistics organizations of which you are a member require only that you pay annual dues, correct?

A: In the case of those organizations, that's true.

Q: Are you familiar with an organization called the International Association for Identification?

A: Yes.

Q: You are not a member of that organization, correct?

A: That's correct. But that...

13. Q: Thank you, you've answered the question.

14. Q: Now, Dr. Peters, isn't it true that

              Dr. Evan Elpus, a Professor of Linguistics at South Northeastwestern University has written that sound spectrographic technology is still highly unreliable?

    A: That's her belief. I disagree.

    Q: Doctor, there is no licensing agency that gives examinations or certifies someone to engage in voice spectrographic analysis, correct?

    Def. Att: Objection. As the question relates in part to credibility, it is improper on voir dire.

15.   The Court: It goes partly to credibility and partly to foundation. Therefore, counsel may ask it.

    A: That's correct.

16.   Q: Lastly, defendant Atlas Insurance has paid you $3000 in connection with your testimony, correct?

    A: For my time in conducting the tests and testifying, yes.

    Pl. Att: No further questions. We would argue that the lack of publications and the lack of the equivalent of Board certification for medical doctors renders the witness unqualified.

    The Court: Anything further from the defense by way of foundation?

    Def. Att: Nothing else. Submitted.

17.   The Court: I rule that the witness is qualified to testify as an expert in voice spectrographic analysis. Defense counsel may resume questioning.

<u>Continued Direct Examination by Defense Counsel</u>

Q: Doctor, please tell us what material you were asked to examine in this case.

A: Certainly. I was given two tapes. One I understood was conceded to have been made by a Wilma Widower about nine years ago. That tape consisted of the message, "Is this working alright? Hi, we love you. We heard about your new car and we're green with envy. We hope to see it and you real soon. Wood and the kids want to say hello so I'll get off. Bye."
The tape containing the voice of an unknown speaker consisted of the message, "I am alright. I see you have painted the house green and gotten a new red car. Love to you and the kids. Goodbye."

Q: Based on your analysis, do you have an opinion as to whether the voices on both tapes are the same?

A: I do.

Q: And what is that opinion?

Pl. Att: Objection, lack of foundation. The witness has not testified to his method of analysis or the basis of his opinion.

18. The Court: Unnecessary. The witness may answer.

A: My opinion is that the voices on the tape are of the same person.

Pl. Att: Objection, that's for the jury to determine, not this witness.

19. The Court: Well, it's proper.

Q: Have you verified this opinion?

20. A: Yes. As I often do, I reviewed my findings with a colleague of mine in

the Phonetics Laboratory, Dr. Flo Tiller. She examined the spectrograms and agreed totally with my conclusions.

Q: Did you consult anyone in addition to Dr. Tiller?

A: Yes, I did. As many linguistic analysts do, and as I instruct my students to do, in forming my opinion I relied partly on the opinion of someone other than an interested party who knew the person very well. In this case, I played the tapes for Norman Bates, who I understand had worked with Wilma for over 5 years. Bates told me that in his opinion, both tapes contained Wilma's voice.

Pl. Att: Objection and move to strike, hearsay.

21. The Court: Sustained.

Pl. Att: Also move to strike this witness' testimony, on the ground that in forming his opinion he has relied on information which the court has ruled improper.

The Court: Dr. Peters, let me ask you this. I have ruled that you cannot consider anything you may have learned from Norman Bates. Without that information, are you still able to form an opinion concerning the identity of voices on the tapes?

A: Oh, yes. That's more in the nature of a double-check.

22. The Court: I rule that Dr. Peters may testify. But Dr. Peters, I caution you not to make reference to or rely in any way on anything you learned from Norman Bates, and I instruct the jurors to disregard that testimony.

Pl. Att: Then Your Honor, we move for a

mistrial. The jurors cannot help but be influenced by having heard what Norman Bates said, which Your Honor has now ruled inadmissible.

23. The Court: Motion denied. Defense counsel may resume testimony.

    Q: Disregarding anything you may have learned from Norman Bates, how confident are you that in this case your opinion is correct?

    Pl. Att: Objection, vague and irrelevant.

24. The Court: No, I'll allow it.

    A: Well, there's always some element of uncertainty, here in particular because the messages contain relatively few words in common. But I am very confident that my opinion is correct.

25. Q: Would you say that your confidence in your opinion is beyond a preponderance of the evidence?

    A: Most certainly.

    Q: Doctor, can you briefly describe how you arrived at your opinion?

    Pl. Att: Objection, vague and calls for a narrative.

26. The Court: Sustained.

    Q: Well, can you tell us what a sound spectrograph is?

    A: It is a machine that converts short segments of speech into visual printouts called spectrograms. A single printout represents about two seconds of speech, so lengthy oral messages might require a large number of spectrograms.

    Q: And what do spectrograms depict?

A: The three principal properties of speech. The first is the time over which a speech sound occurs; that is represented on a horizontal axis from left to right on a spectrogram. The second is the frequency or pitch of a sound; that is shown on the vertical axis. The higher the frequency, the higher the markings along the vertical axis. Finally there's loudness. The louder a sound, the darker its depiction on the spectrogram.

27. Q: Your Honor, I have a transparency which I've shown to plaintiff's counsel and which I'd ask to be marked defense Exhibit A. It consists of two nearly identical spectrograms, one above the other. The top one depicts the word "green" in the earlier tape, the lower one depicts the same word "green" in the later tape.

Q: Doctor Peters, I hand you Exhibit A and ask if you recognize it as a transparency which you prepared from the original spectrograms of the word "green" in each of the taped messages.

Pl. Att: Objection, leading.

28. The Court: Overruled.

A: Yes, it is.

Q: How do you recognize it?

A: It's stamped with my initials in the lower left hand corner, and I've noted the tapes from which the transparency was made.

Q: Can you compare the two spectrograms for us?

Pl. Att: May I have brief voir dire as to the authenticity of the transparency?

The Court: Make it brief.

Voir Dire Examination by Plaintiff's Counsel

Q: Dr. Peters, was Exhibit A prepared in the Phonetics Lab at NYUCLA?

A: Yes.

29. Q: That's an area to which many students have access, correct?

A: Yes.

Q: And your initials are stamped on, not written by you personally?

A: That's my procedure, yes.

Q: You usually keep this stamp on top of your desk?

A: That's correct.

30. Q: So that any student who perhaps has been paid a little something can just come along with a transparency that they've made, stamp your initials on it and you wouldn't know anything about it?

A: That's highly unlikely. Besides, I personally noted the tapes from which the transparency was made.

Pl. Att: I object that the authentication is insufficient.

31. The Court: Overruled. And as my ruling is final, I instruct the jury that it must accept the transparency as authentic. Continue the direct examination.

Continued Direct Examination by Defense Counsel

Q: Dr. Peters, I ask you again to compare the two spectrograms.

Pl. Att: Objection based on the original

writing rule. The spectrogram itself, not this witness' testimony, is the best evidence of its contents.

32. The Court: Overruled; you may answer.

   A: There are two characteristics which suggest very strongly that the voices on both tapes are the same. Note first that in terms of frequency, this portion here, which represents the "r" sound, is very low on the vertical axis on both spectrograms. Second, note that in the "gr" sound, there is a very similar and lengthy time duration between the "g" and the "r." This is a highly idiosyncratic speech pattern.

   Q: So that the record is clear, let me indicate that when referring to the portion of the spectrograms which depict the "r" sound, the witness pointed to markings that are about a third of the way across each spectrogram reading from left to right, an area about half an inch wide and an inch high.

   Pl. Att: Objection. Counsel is testifying.

33. The Court: What ruling?

   Q: Also for purposes of a clear record, let me indicate that the witness testified that the time duration between the "g" and "r" sounds on both spectrograms was also very idiosyncratic.

   Pl. Att: Same objection.

34. The Court: What ruling?

   Q: Next, let me turn your attention to a second transparency...

   (Remainder of testimony concerning the expert's comparisons of the taped messages and introduction of the transparencies and tapes into evidence omitted.)

Q: Dr. Peters, in your opinion is it possible for one person to mimic another's voice to such an extent that they would produce very similar spectrograms?

Pl. Att: Objection, irrelevant. We have not offered evidence of attempted mimicry.

35. The Court: Well, the jurors may have that concern themselves. I'll permit it.

A: No. Many studies have been done using professional mimics. Even though some of them have been able to imitate another's verbal style, their spectrograms are always very different.

36. Q: Just to conclude, then, Dr. Peters, please state once more your opinion regarding the voices on the two tapes.

A: My opinion is that they are the voices of the same speaker.

Cross Examination of Dr. Ian Peters by Plaintiff's Counsel

Q: Dr. Peters, isn't it true that you've never offered a course on the use of the sound spectrograph to identify speakers?

Def. Att: Objection, irrelevant. The question pertains to the witness' qualifications as an expert.

37. The Court: Since it's also relevant to credibility, I'll allow it.

A: Yes, that is true.

Q: You normally use the spectrograph to compare speech sounds among speakers of different languages?

A: That is true, yes.

Q: Now, a number of computer-based systems for analyzing speech sounds are available, correct?

Def. Att: Objection, beyond the scope of direct. I asked nothing about computer-based systems.

The Court: Will both counsel come up to the sidebar for an offer of proof?

Pl. Att: I intend to cast doubt on the accuracy of Dr. Peters' opinion by showing that he failed to employ any of a number of computer-based systems for differentiating speech sounds that are available in the doctor's own laboratory.

38. The Court: Defense counsel asked nothing about computer-based programs. The objection is sustained. You may return to counsel table; we will proceed with cross examination.

Q: Doctor, are you familiar with the report of the National Academy of Sciences entitled "On the Theory and Practice of Voice Identification?"

A: I am.

Q: I show you what has previously been marked as Plaintiff's Exhibit 3 for identification; I have shown it to defense counsel. Is Exhibit 3 a copy of the National Academy report?

A: It appears to be, yes.

Q: Do you consider the report a reliable analysis of voice identification?

A: I can't say that I agree with all of it, but for the most part I would say it is reliable.

Q: Let me read you a passage...

Def. Att: Might I take the witness on voir dire?

The Court: Well, be brief.

Voir Dire Examination by Defense Counsel

Q: Dr. Peters, did you consider the report in arriving at your opinion in this case?

A: If you mean did I consult it, no.

Q: Did you rely on it in any way?

A: No.

Def. Att: I object to counsel's asking the witness anything from that report.

39. The Court: For me to allow the question, it must be shown to my satisfaction that the report is reliable.

40. The Court: I will permit plaintiff's counsel to question the witness by reading portions of the report to him.

Continued Cross Examination by Plaintiff's Counsel

Q: Dr. Peters, reading from page 85, the report states, does it not, that "identification error rates are higher for noncontemporaneous samples?"

A: That is true.

Q: And here a nine year gap separates the tapes?

A: I'm told that's the case. I personally would have no way of knowing, of course.

41. Q: So even though you think the National Academy's report is wrong about the effect of a gap, you still accept it as a reliable authority?

A: A gap between recordings is but one variable which may affect the accuracy of identification. In this case, other circumstances existed which enabled me to conclude that they were the same voice.

Q: Your Honor, I will now read into the record from page 102 of the report, which states, "Virtually all voicegram experiments have used adult male speakers."

Def. Att: Objection and move to strike, counsel must ask questions, not make statements.

42. The Court: What ruling?

Q: I would also mark as an exhibit and offer into evidence as Plaintiff's Exhibit 4, page 10 of the report. Exhibit 4 contains the statement, "At the present time, the technique of voice identification lacks a solid theoretical basis for demonstrating that intraspeaker variability is less than interspeaker variability."

43. The Court: What response to the request?

Q: Now, you are familiar with Dr. Gary Asimow, correct?

A: Yes, Dr. Asimow is one of the preeminent researchers in the field of linguistics.

Q: You regard him as reliable?

A: Yes indeed.

44. Q: And isn't it true that based on spectrographic analysis of the tapes in this case, Dr. Asimow concluded that they contain the voices of different people?

A: That's correct; on this matter, we have differing opinions.

Q: Doctor, in addition to doing the spectrographic analysis which you've described, your opinion as to whether the voices are the same is also based in part on listening to the tapes, correct?

Def. Att: Objection, assumes facts not in evidence. I elicited no information about whether Dr. Peters listened to the tapes.

45. The Court: Even if I accept that that is true, your objection is overruled.

A: Yes, that is part of my professional examination.

Q: You listen to the tapes and make a judgment as to whether the voices are the same?

A: Well, a preliminary judgment. I may not even do the spectrographic analysis if in my opinion the voices are too dissimilar. But certainly this is one factor in my opinion.

Q: Dr. Peters, I have here two tapes. Each contains a voice reciting a different one of the messages that you analyzed in this case. I'll play the two tapes, and then I'd like you to tell the jurors whether the voices are of the same person.

46. Def. Att: Does defense counsel have grounds to object? If so, what are they?

47. Q: Doctor, while you were a graduate student you were put on probation for a semester for plagiarizing a term paper, correct?

A: I don't remember, that would have been years ago.

48. Q: Let me show you Plaintiff's Exhibit 5, which I've marked for identification

and shown to defense counsel. Is this a copy of a notice you received while pursuing your M.A. at Oxford placing you on probation for plagiarizing a term paper?

A: I do remember that now. An error of youth, I'm afraid.

Q: Doctor, are you aware that the International Association of Voice Identification recommends that an opinion as to voice identity should be based on a sample of no fewer than 10 words in common?

Def. Att: Objection, hearsay.

49. The Court: Overruled.

A: Yes, I am aware of that.

Q: That's an organization of which you're not a member, correct?

Def. Att: Objection, plaintiff's counsel has already asked that question and received an answer.

50. The Court: Sustained.

Q: The messages on which you base your opinion in this case had only seven words in common, correct?

A: That is correct.

51. Q: Earlier you disregarded the recommendations of the National Academy of Sciences, now you're disregarding the views of the International Association of Voice Identification, and yet you think the jurors ought to believe you?

A: As I've tried to explain, no one factor is determinative. Given the quality of the recordings and the types of similarities, there was sufficient data for me to conclude that the voices were the same.

    Pl. Att: Object and move to strike, non-responsive. The question called for a simple "yes" or "no" answer.

52. The Court: What ruling?

    Pl. Att: No further questions at this time.

    The Court: Redirect?

    Def. Att: Very briefly, Your Honor.

Redirect Examination by Defense Counsel

53. Q: Doctor, would you say that your opinion is based on a combination of the duration of the messages, the number of similarities, and the quality of the recordings?

    A: Yes.

    Q: No further questions.

Chapter 10

A Final Transcript

Transcript No. 19

Testimony

In the Matter of Turney

This is an administrative disciplinary hearing initiated by the petitioner State Bar. The State Bar seeks disciplinary sanctions against one of its members, respondent Anna Turney, for acting without the authority of and attempting to induce perjury by a former client, Rhea Taylor. Specifically, the State Bar contends that Turney had represented Taylor in a breach of lease action brought against Taylor by Phil Emall Development Co., and that Turney had acted without authority in defending the action and had urged Taylor to submit a false declaration as part of an opposition to a summary judgment motion filed by Emall. Turney denies both allegations.

You are to assume that (1) if true, the State Bar charges constitute actions for which the attorney may be properly disciplined; (2) the Federal Rules of Evidence apply in this State Bar disciplinary hearing; and (3) respondent has the right to and has requested a jury trial. The petitioner's first witness is Rhea Taylor.

Direct Examination of Rhea Taylor by Counsel for Petitioner

Q: Ms. Taylor, what is your occupation?

A: I own retail guitar shops. I have 3 shops here in town.

Q: Do you know a lawyer by the name of Anna Turney?

A: Yes, I hired her to represent me when I was sued for breach of a lease agreement.

1. Q: Please describe the circumstances which resulted in your hiring Ms. Turney to represent you.

   A: Certainly. In mid-March of last year I had some discussions with Phil Emall about leasing store space in a new shopping mall that Emall was just about to open. I decided to sign a lease and open what would be my fourth store. Unfortunately, within a few weeks after I had signed the lease the retail guitar business really went sour and I realized that I could not afford to open a new store.

   Q: By the way, did this lease that you signed have any language concerning whether a department store had agreed to be a tenant in the mall?

   Resp. Att: Objection. Counsel must either produce the lease itself or explain its absence.

2. The Court: I'll allow the witness to answer.

   A: No, it didn't.

   Q: What then happened?

   A: After thinking it over, I contacted someone in Emall's office and told him that I could not go through with the lease, that I wanted to do business with Emall in the future, and that I hoped Emall would just let me out of the lease.

   Resp. Att: Might I take the witness on voir dire?

   The Court: Very briefly.

   Resp. Att: Did you send Emall anything in writing indicating your withdrawal from the lease?

A: Yes, the same day that I talked to his assistant I sent Emall a cancellation letter.

Resp. Att: Objection to what the witness told the assistant based on the Original Writing Rule, Your Honor. The letter to Emall is the best evidence of what she told Emall.

3. The Court: Overruled. Petitioner's counsel may resume questioning.

4. Q: Ms. Taylor, I am marking as Petitioner's 1 and showing to respondent's counsel what appears to be a letter from Phil Emall indicating his intention to hold you to the lease agreement, dated April 10 of last year. Did you receive this letter after you sent your letter to Emall?

A: I did.

Q: Do you recognize Petitioner's 1?

A: It's the letter I got from Emall Development Company, though I can't say I've seen Mr. Emall's signature enough to recognize this as his signature.

Q: Your Honor, I ask that Petitioner's 1 be received in evidence, and ask permission to read its contents to the jury.

5. The Court: What ruling?

Q: What then happened?

A: I decided to call Emall personally and make another try to work things out. But it was no go. He said that he was sorry to take a hardball position, but that if I didn't go through with the lease he would sue for damages.

Resp. Att: Objection to what Emall said, hearsay.

Pet. Att: This is non-hearsay, Your Honor, offered to prove the basis of the dispute which led Ms. Taylor to contact Turney.

6. The Court: Objection overruled.

Q: Did Mr. Emall say anything else?

A: Yes, he said wouldn't drop it because he thought that I wanted to cancel the lease only because I wanted to get a better deal in another location.

Resp. Att: Objection, lack of personal knowledge and speculation on Emall's part.

7. The Court: What ruling?

Q: How did matters stand following this conversation?

A: I told him that I had to do what was best for my business, and not rent the space. I pointed out that he still had time to find another tenant before the mall opened.

Q: And did Emall rent the store space you were to occupy?

8. A: Yes, but for less than half the amount of rent that I was supposed to pay.

9. Q: Why didn't Mr. Emall make an effort to lease the space for the same rent you were to have paid?

10. A: He was angry that I broke the lease and he thought he'd get back at me by sticking me with the difference in rent.

11. Q: Ms. Taylor, the following June 10, you consulted with Anna Turney after you were served with a complaint for breach of a lease agreement filed by Mr. Emall?

A: Yes.

Q: Had Ms. Turney represented you previously?

A: No. But I talked to a business associate about my problem with Mr. Emall, and he recommended Turney as someone I'd have to watch carefully, but who could be aggressive if need be.

Resp. Att: Objection and move to strike, hearsay.

12. The Court: What ruling?

Q: Now, what if anything caught your eye when you first entered Turney's office?

13. A: The disorder. Her desk was extremely messy, half the floor area was covered with papers, and in one corner of the room on the floor I noticed a shot glass.

14. Q: Did you provide Ms. Turney with the information you've just testified to?

A: That's correct.

Q: Did you say anything else?

A: Yes, I told Ms. Turney that I was still hopeful of doing future business with Emall, so that if at all possible I wanted things to work out on friendly terms.

Resp. Att: Objection, hearsay.

15. The Court: Overruled. The witness is only testifying to what she herself said.

Q: How did Ms. Turney respond?

16. A: She said that Emall probably had a solid breach of contract claim, but

that we could definitely fight him on damages and maybe some other issues. She said she'd think about it further and get back to me in a couple of days.

Q: Did Ms. Turney discuss fees with you during this meeting?

A: Yes, I agreed to pay fees per her usual hourly charge.

Q: Did you discuss anything else during this initial meeting?

A: Yes, Ms. Turney said we could either take a conciliatory approach by conceding liability and trying to negotiate damages, or take an aggressive approach and make it as expensive as possible for Emall to continue the suit. She strongly urged me to take the latter course as a way of keeping Emall's respect.

Resp. Att: Objection, irrelevant. The only possible relevance of this testimony is to suggest that Ms. Turney was unfairly trying to maximize her fees, and that is an offense with which she is not charged.

17. The Court: Overruled.

18. Resp. Att: As respondent's attorney, is any other objection to the last answer available?

Q: How did you respond to this advice?

A: I said I'd think it over.

19. Q: How would you have responded if Ms. Turney had advised a conciliatory approach?

A: I'm sure I would have readily agreed. Frankly, at the time that made more sense to me.

Q: Can you recall anything else that took place during that initial meeting?

A: No, that's about it.

Q: Now, did Turney call you back in a couple of days, as promised?

A: No, over a week went by, and it was me who finally called her back.

Resp. Att: Objection, irrelevant.

20. The Court: What ruling?

Q: The next time you spoke with her was about June 17?

A: That's correct.

21. Q: OK, please describe this conversation.

A: Well, Ms. Turney said that she had talked to a Joe Bashout, who was Emall's attorney. She said that to check Bashout's attitude, she had argued that the lease was unenforceable because there was no guarantee that the mall was going to open on schedule. Bashout said he thought that there was no merit to that argument and that he wouldn't discuss it further.

Resp. Att: Objection to Bashout's statement, hearsay.

22. The Court: Overruled.

Q: Please continue.

A: Ms. Turney said we had to respond to the complaint. I said I was still uncertain about what to do, and asked if she could get more time. She said she thought that was a mistake, but that she could try.

23. Q: At any time during this conversation, did you authorize Ms. Turney to file an answer?

A: No, I did not.

Q: In either the June 10 or the June 17 conversation, did you ever discuss a statement by Emall that a department store was going to be a mall tenant?

A: No, he never said any such thing.

24. Q: How is it you are certain of that?

A: Just as soon as I got through talking to Turney, I prepared a memo of our conversation for my records.

Q: Why did you do that?

25. A: The same business associate who recommended Ms. Turney also told me that once I got involved in litigation I should keep accurate records of all documents and conversations. I'm glad I did; now I know what my friend meant by having to watch Turney carefully.

Pet. Att: I have marked as Petitioner's 2 and shown to respondent's attorney a document dated June 22. May I approach the witness? Thank you. Ms. Taylor, please look over petitioner's 2 and tell us if you recognize it.

A: Yes, this appears to be the memo I prepared.

26. Q: This is your handwriting?

A: Yes.

Pet. Att: I ask that Petitioner's 2 be received in evidence.

Resp. Att: Objection, hearsay.

27. The Court: What ruling?

28. Q: Next, showing you this answer titled <u>Emall Development Co. v. Taylor</u>, did you ever see this before it was filed?

   A: No.

29. Q: As you see, the answer includes an affirmative defense that Emall induced you to enter into the lease by making fraudulent misrepresentations. What did you do after you noticed that?

   A: I put a call in to Ms. Turney to ask why she had filed an answer. She said she was afraid she might not get an extension of time so she went ahead and filed the answer. She also said something about it just protecting my rights.

30. Q: Ms. Turney didn't check with you before filing it even though she knew that you were available?

   A: That's correct.

   Q: Did you have any further discussion of the answer?

31. A: I said I was still upset. I mentioned that I'd just read about how many attorneys were having drug problems that led them to give poor representation, and that I hoped nothing like that was going on. She denied having any drug problems.

   Q: Now, I'd like to call your attention to mid-December of last year, about 6 months after you spoke to Ms. Turney about the answer. Do you recall talking to Ms. Turney about this case at that time?

   A: I do.

   Q: What took place at that time?

   A: She told me that Emall had asked for something called summary judgment.

She said that I had to sign a paper giving a good reason why the lease was invalid or we'd lose the case.

Q: Go on.

A: I asked what we could do. She said that she had anticipated this when she filed the answer. She told me that if I stated that Emall had made some promise to me before I signed the lease, we could win the case.

Q: What did you say to that?

A: I said I couldn't think of anything. She said she'd take care of it by saying that Emall had told me that a department store had agreed to lease space. She said they'd have a hell of a time proving it wasn't true, and that it would block summary judgment.

Q: Can you recall her exact words?

Resp. Att: Objection, asked and answered.

32. The Court: Overruled, witness may answer.

A: I remember that she said, "We'll say Emall said that Nerdstroms has agreed to be a tenant. That sounds good."

Q: How did you respond?

A: I said, "Oh my God, you're asking me to commit perjury. You must do this all the time." She said, "Those are your words, not mine."

Resp. Att: Objection, hearsay.

33. The Court: I can admit the witness' assertion as an excited utterance if the jury could reasonably believe that it was made under the stress of excitement.

34. The Court: Though I believe that the jury

189

could reasonably believe that the statement was made under the stress of excitement, I rule that the assertion is too conclusory to be admissible as Taylor's excited utterance.

35. The Court: However, I may also admit the assertion as Turney's admission if the jury could reasonably construe Turney's response as an adoption of Taylor's statement.

36. The Court: I admit Taylor's statement as Turney's admission.

Q: How did you respond to that?

A: That made me really upset. I shouted to her about how lawyers like her were screwing up our whole system of justice and she ought to be disbarred. Then I fired her.

Resp. Att: Objection and move to strike. Hearsay and irrelevant.

37. The Court: The witness was clearly still under the stress of excitement. I'll allow it.

Q: Did Ms. Turney respond?

38. A: Yes, she said that I was the second client in 3 months who had fired her just because she was doing everything she could to help them.

Q: Nothing further at this time.

Cross Examination by Respondent's Attorney

Q: Ms. Taylor, prior to retaining Ms. Turney in this matter, your litigation had been handled by another attorney, Sydney Bernard, correct?

Pet. Att: Objection, irrelevant.

Resp. Att: This is foundational to showing

that Ms. Taylor herself suggested the idea of perjury, Your Honor.

Pet. Att: Nevertheless, Your Honor, the independent relevance of this question has not been shown.

39. The Court: Objection overruled.

A: That's true, yes.

Q: And the reason you did not retain Mr. Bernard in this matter is because you thought that he was not rough and nasty enough in a previous case?

Pet. Att: Objection, vague.

40. The Court: Overruled.

A: No, that's not right. I didn't think he had pursued a previous case very aggressively.

Q: But you told Ms. Turney that you wanted a lawyer who could play rough and nasty if necessary?

Pet. Att: Objection, improper impeachment.

41. The Court: I can admit the evidence of Taylor's out of court statement upon making a final determination that the alleged statement to Turney is inconsistent with Taylor's in-court testimony.

42. The Court: I'll allow the question for impeachment purposes only.

A: I'm sure I didn't say that.

Resp. Att: For the Court's information, I intend to bring out during the testimony of Ms. Turney that Ms. Taylor did make this statement to her.

The Court: What is the relevance, counsel?

Resp. Att: A client who, like Ms. Taylor,

says that she is interested in an attorney who can play rough and nasty is more likely to suggest perjury than a client who does not say such things.

Pet. Att: That's nonsense, Your Honor. Even if for the sake of argument we assume that Ms. Taylor said that, surely all clients who say they want rough and nasty attorneys do not want to commit perjury. Ms. Turney's testimony would be collateral.

43. The Court: Would you allow Turney to testify to Taylor's remark?

Q: Ms. Taylor, when you consulted Ms. Turney, you did so because you wanted an aggressive attorney, isn't that right?

Pet. Att: Objection, asked and answered. The witness gave this testimony on direct and already on cross.

44. The Court: Well, this is cross examination. I'll allow the question.

A: Yes, that's true, but I still wanted to keep open the possibility of future dealings with Emall.

Resp. Att: Move to strike everything after "I did" as non-responsive.

45. The Court: Motion granted. The jury is to disregard the last comment.

Q: You felt you could not afford to open a new store?

A: That's true.

Q: In fact, if you had to live up to the lease you may well have lost all of your stores, isn't that right?

Pet. Att: Objection. Counsel is putting words that she never testified to into the witness' mouth.

46. The Court: Overruled.

   A: A new store would have been a financial burden, but I didn't think I'd lose my whole business if that's what you mean.

47. Q: You're asking the jury to believe that you're making phone calls, sending letters and contacting attorneys to get out of a lease that you had just signed but that you weren't afraid of losing your entire business?

   A: Well, that's the way it was.

48. Q: Isn't it a fact that it was you, and not Ms. Turney, who suggested that you prepare a declaration falsely stating that Emall had induced you to sign a lease by saying a Nerdstroms department store had already agreed to become a tenant in the mall?

   A: No, that's not true.

49. Q: Moving on, Ms. Taylor, last year a customer named Sossin was successful in a civil action against you because you misrepresented a guitar as having been once owned by George Harrison, correct?

   A: No, that's not true.

   Resp. Att: I have here, marked as Respondent's Exhibit "A," an Abstract of Judgment in Sossin v. Taylor, reciting a finding of fraud by defendant Taylor and awarding judgment to Sossin in the amount of $13,000. I ask that it be received in evidence.

50. The Court: What ruling?

   Q: And two years ago you were convicted of willful failure to pay child support, isn't that true?

   Pet. Att: Objection, improper character

evidence.

51. The Court: Since the witness' character is not in issue, the question would be proper only if failure to pay child support is either a felony or a crime involving dishonesty or false statement.

52. The Court: Respondent's counsel has the burden of convincing me by clear and convincing evidence that the crime of which Ms. Taylor was allegedly convicted was a felony or involved false statement or dishonesty.

Resp. Att: By way of offer of proof, we're prepared to show that Ms. Taylor evaded her child support obligation for 2 years by lying about her earnings.

The Court: Anything further by way of offer of proof?

Resp. Att: No, that's it.

53. The Court: My ruling is that the question constitutes improper impeachment. Let's move on.

Q: No further questions at this time.

After the presentation of additional evidence, the petitioner rested its case. Respondent made a motion to dismiss out of the presence of the jury; the motion was denied. Anna Turney was then called to the stand to testify in her own behalf.

Direct Examination of Anna Turney by Respondent's Attorney

Q: Ms. Turney, how long have you been practicing law?

A: For about 15 years.

Q: What type of practice do you have?

A: I've been a sole practitioner for about seven years. I have a general commercial practice.

Q: Were you in a different kind of practice before you became a sole practitioner?

54. A: Before that, I was a legal services attorney doing mainly law reform litigation on behalf of children.

Q: Did you receive any awards while a legal services attorney?

55. A: Yes. Two years before I went into private practice, I received the County Bar Annual Award for my work as a children's rights advocate.

56. Q: Have you ever been sanctioned by the State Bar for breach of professional duties?

A: No.

Q: Since becoming a sole practitioner, have you done any lecturing?

57. A: Yes. Twice a year I teach a course for practicing attorneys on the subject of professional responsibility, for which attorneys get continuing education credit.

Q: Ms. Turney, let me take you back to your initial meeting with Ms. Taylor. Do you recall that meeting?

A: Yes I do.

Q: What was the problem for which she was seeking your help?

Pet. Att: Objection, we've already been through this. Cumulative.

58. The Court: Overruled.

A: She said that she had been served with a complaint because she had signed a lease which she could no longer afford to enter into. Her business, retail sales of guitars, was in such a big slump that she had felt forced to back out of a lease, and she was worried that if she had to pay a lot of damages she could be forced into bankruptcy. After talking to her and looking over her papers, I told her that my initial impression was that she didn't have much of a defense on liability, but that the landlord's damage claim was very questionable.

Pet. Att: Objection, hearsay; move to strike.

59. The Court: What ruling?

Q: What was her frame of mind while she was talking with you?

60. A: She was extremely nervous. At one point she got so anxious that I stopped the interview and gave her a glass of fruit juice to help her calm down.

Q: You say she was nervous. Can you be more specific?

61. A: Oh, I remember she fidgeted a lot, asked me to repeat myself a few times, and spoke very tensely and sometimes barely audibly. She also repeatedly asked for reassurance that there was a way to defeat Emall's claim.

Q: What if any advice did you give her?

Pet. Att: Objection, hearsay. The witness is testifying to her own out of court statement.

62. The Court: Overruled, goes to Ms. Taylor's state of mind.

A: I advised Ms. Taylor that she could take either a conciliatory or an aggressive defense posture. Being conciliatory, we could concede liability and try to negotiate damages. Being aggressive, we'd try to contest everything we legally could. I told her that she didn't have to decide that day, but to call me back in a day or two. In the meantime, I said I'd call Emall's attorney.

Q: When did you next hear from her?

A: Nearly a week later. She said that a friend had reminded her that before she signed the lease, Emall had said that Nerdstroms had agreed to be a tenant in the mall. Ms. Taylor said that was false, there was no department store in the mall. She wanted to know that if this is what had happened, would she have good defense to Emall's suit.

Pet. Att: Object and move to strike, hearsay of both the friend and Ms. Taylor.

63. The Court: What ruling?

64. Q: You are quite clear that it was Ms. Taylor who first mentioned Emall's statement that Nerdstroms had agreed to be a mall tenant?

A: Absolutely.

Q: What did you say?

65. A: I said that if that was the case, we could file an answer which contested both liability and damages. She said that's just what had happened, and she then authorized me to file an such an answer, and I did.

Q: What happened next?

(portion of testimony omitted)

Q: Ms. Turney, since these events, have you spoken to people about Ms. Taylor?

A: Yes, to many people in the wholesale and retail guitar and music business.

Q: Are you aware of whether she has a reputation as an honest person?

A: Yes.

Q: And what is that reputation?

Pet. Att: Objection, lack of foundation.

66. The Court: The foundation is adequate so long as there is evidence from which the jury can reasonably conclude that this witness is aware of Ms. Taylor's reputation.

67. The Court: Even if the foundation is adequate, the testimony is improper character evidence.

68. Q: Based on your contact with her in this matter, do you have an opinion as to Ms. Taylor's honesty?

A: Yes, in my opinion she is not truthful.

Q: Did you learn anything else about Ms. Taylor?

69. A: Yes. I found out that once before, Ms. Taylor had sued an attorney for ethical violations and lost.

Q: Nothing further.

Cross Examination of Anna Turney by Petitioner's Attorney

Q: Ms. Turney, isn't it true that you filed the answer without notifying Ms. Taylor in advance?

A: No, that's not true.

69. Q: Let me refer you to what has previously been marked Petitioner's "3," the deposition of Rhea Taylor. On page 107, lines 12-14, she testified that she did not know that you had filed an answer, correct?

A: Yes, she said that.

Q: Ms. Turney, you previously had represented a client in a suit against Mr. Emall for improperly conducting an environmental impact study, correct?

A: Yes.

70. Q: And Mr. Emall filed a complaint with the State Bar claiming that you verbally abused his employees, correct?

(Answer and remainder of cross omitted)

APPENDIX

Transcript 1
(State v. David Gillig)

The purpose of this chapter is to introduce a few basic evidentiary concepts. Transcript 1 focuses on the oath. It should enable you to understand that even though the FRE abolishes all common law competency requirements except in a few diversity actions, and even though Rule 603 says only that witnesses must take an oath, most judges still consider it foundational that a witness is able to understand the oath. One area where the issue surfaces is with young children.

1. How does Jimmy know he's 6 years old? How does any of us know how old we are, aside from what we are told? This suggests a problem known as "hearsay:" testifying to information that we've heard from other people. In this context, the hearsay problem is one that courts almost always ignore, otherwise there is little that any witness could say. After all, someone probably told us what color "red" is too.

2. An attorney's role on direct is basically to ask questions that elicit testimony about what happened, but an attorney is usually allowed some leeway to make a preliminary statement to "relax" a child or other nervous witness. However, you might think this statement goes a bit too far in suggesting that Jimmy say the same thing he's said before.

3. and 4. These raise "foundational" issues; see FRE 104. The question of Jimmy's ability to understand the oath is foundational to his testimony. When there is a preliminary issue to decide who decides, and by what standard? Both of the court's statements are correct; the latter is well within its discretion. (Note that the FRE are apparently silent on which party has the burden of establishing a foundational issue which the judge decides.)

5. The defense attorney should move to strike everything after "Yes" as non-responsive.

6. The ruling is partially correct. As is all too typical with children, Jimmy seems definitely committed to telling the truth when questioned by friendly counsel, and less certain when questioned by a stranger. In view of Jimmy's seeming understanding of what a lie is, and what the oath means, the ruling seems within the judge's discretion. However, the judge has articulated the wrong standard of proof. Competency, like other foundations, need be shown only by a preponderance of the evidence.

Transcript 2
(State v. David Gillig (cont'd.))

This transcript concerns a second basic concept of proof, personal knowledge. It illustrates the difference between uncertainty and pure guesswork. If a witness is unsure, a judge will usually allow the testimony, on the theory that the uncertainty goes only to the weight of the testimony. That should apply to the various ways in which this witness is uncertain. (Nos. 1, 2, 4, 8) On the other hand, when a witness seems to genuinely lack personal knowledge, and gives a guess or speculates, a judge is likely to rule the testimony inadmissible. (No. 6)

3. While it is often hard to distinguish among objections that a witness "lacks personal knowledge," is "speculating," or that a "question calls for a conclusion," this probably belongs in the "speculation" category.

5. Based on everyday personal experience, witnesses are usually allowed to give opinions (state conclusions) such as, "She was smiling (or frowning, happy, sad, etc.)." It would simply be impossible for most witnesses to describe the individual facial characteristics which would allow a trier of fact to conclude that someone was "smiling." But even adults are unlikely to be experienced in distinguishing real from phony smiles. Thus, the witness "lacks personal knowledge" (or "is speculating." or...) Note also that attorney shouldn't make statements.

6. How does Jimmy know that pictures were being taken? Maybe the camera had no film in it. Should the witness only be allowed to say, "He held the camera up to his eye and pressed a button 10 times?"

7. An attorney is not foreclosed by a witness' claim of inability to remember. Attorneys can ask additional questions. As here, and especially with a child, the question can even be leading. Note, however, that there is no showing that the witness knows what the term "privates" refers to. Should the defense

attorney ask to take the witness on voir dire to explore this? Note the tactical issues that can confront lawyers in trial. As the testimony unfolded, the defense attorney was not hurt: Jimmy remembered nothing about his privates. A voir dire exploration of the meaning of the term might have refreshed Jimmy's recollection.

9. The Court has correctly stated the legal standard. (FRE 104 (b))

10. Probably enough personal knowledge has been shown to get the testimony to the jury: the information elicited on cross goes to the weight only. (Note that the defense gets 2 chances to knock out Jimmy's testimony- one before the judge on a legal issue, another before the jury on a credibility issue.)

Transcript 3
(Huston v. Dobbs)

1. In the view of many judges, questions to witnesses (at least non-expert witnesses) are supposed to be narrowly cast. A narrow question tells opposing counsel what sort of response is likely to emerge, giving opposing counsel a chance to object before a statement which might be both inadmissible and prejudicial escapes a witness' lips. In addition, narrow questions might save time, by discouraging witnesses from launching into irrelevant sideroads.

On the other hand, attorneys often want witnesses to describe events without constant interruption by questions, and in their own words. By doing so, it is often thought, enhances a witness' overall credibility.

This question is rather open-ended, and in many judges' eyes would impermissibly "call for a narrative answer." One way to render it less objectionable would be to narrow its time focus: "Describe the condition of the hotel when you first arrived there." Or, one might narrow the physical scope: "Describe the condition of your room." Some judges, of course, would allow the question as is, particularly if in previous questioning the witness has shown to be able to stick to the point.

2. Even if it had been allowed, the broad question did not produce the desired result. The response is an impermissible conclusion: we don't know what the witness' standards of comparison are, and the witness has to state underlying details from which the trier can draw its own conclusion. "Hellhole" is an unduly emotive term that could be stricken.

3. A classic leading question. Though it's phrased in a way that it could be answered "yes" or "no," we want this evidence coming from witnesses, not attorneys.

4. Distinguish this question from No. 1. Though open in form, No. 4 is far less likely to be deemed objectionable, as it asks the witness to describe a discrete event.

5. In the midst of an otherwise acceptable answer, the witness throws in what looks like objectionable speculation ("Obviously..."). The point here is for you to recognize that you can object to all or part of an answer, even if the question is OK.

6. The attorney prefaces a valid question asking for more detail with a statement repeating prior testimony. If not overdone, OK as a means of clarifying for witness and trier where in the story one is. Note that the question slightly mischaracterizes the testimony, implying that both rats ran across the room.

7. Students often think that an introductory statement such as this constitutes leading. However, one is allowed to call a witness' attention to the topic on which the witness is to testify.

8. A common problem. The attorney asks two questions, the first one broad and open, the second one narrow. Which one is the witness supposed to answer?

9. Questions assumes facts not in evidence, that complaints had been made.

10. Strike "Let me add..." There is no question pending.

11. The question is vague/unintelligible. We're not in the context of a particular event, so the term "next" has no meaning.

12. Leading, but OK on cross. Basic tool.

13. Again illustrating that portions of answers can be stricken if improper. "He's lying" is non-responsive, and an impermissible opinion.

14. An argumentative question: it's not asking for information. Perhaps the lawyer was goaded by # 13, but lawyers are expected to exercise self-control.

15. While most of the answer seems speculative, most judges will probably allow it since the dumb "why" question seems to invite speculation.

16. Most judges allow a cross examiner to cut off an explanation, at least where the witness has been able to answer the question as asked. As part of the adversary system, they permit each side to make the best case it can.

Transcript 4
(O'Hare v. Hutchinson)

1. Acceptable background question, though strictly speaking not within the definition of relevance. Often allowed on the bases that it relaxes the witness, and gives the trier a chance to become familiar with a witness.

2. This probably goes beyond acceptable background evidence, more into evidence of good character which at this stage is inadmissible.

3. Discussion of # 2 applies here. In addition, the award is plainly irrelevant.

4. While the route is not directly tied to the issue of where O'Hare was struck, this is admissible. Because testimony typically emerges in story form, events before and after the "moment of substantive importance" (MSI) are necessarily included. Also, the evidence shows that Hutchinson has a clear recall of immediately surrounding events, thus potentially bolstering her credibility.

5. Irrelevant. Though students love to ask "usually" questions, how fast she "usually" drives, being a composite of all different situations, is not logically connected to how she was driving on this occasion.

6. The questioner begins by "echoing" the previous answer, a habit most judges find highly irksome and objectionable. The question is probably relevant--how she was driving in the minutes leading up to the accident does have some tendency to prove how she was driving at the MSI.

7. A relevant question. Since most of us believe in cause and effect, an explanation accounting for her speed tends to enhance the credibility of her statement that she was only going 20 m.p.h.

8. Relevant to show familiarity with the scene.

9. Good open question that allows witness to testify in her own words. A minority of judges might regard it as calling for a narrative.

10. Leading. Sometimes judges will allow a question in this form to emphasize testimony already given, but this question goes beyond the witness' answer.

11. The ruling is properly within the trial court's discretion under FRE 104(c).

12. The statement of the legal rule is correct. FRE 104(b). Probably the foundation is sufficient for a finding of personal knowledge, it's a low threshold.

13. The ruling is probably correct--at least well within a trial judge's discretion. How O'Hare might have behaved on a single occasion in the past, even at the same location, is irrelevant, but might be given great weight by the jury. (Note that if it were otherwise admissible, the "I'm pretty sure" is enough for personal knowledge.) On the other hand, the "extra care" Hutchinson might have taken seems pretty minimal, as jaywalkers are a rather common sight.

14. The Court would have discretion to grant this request, though if it thought the connection between seeing a jaywalker a week earlier and driving carefully very weak, it might well deny it, as here.
   Note that as frequently occurs, the jurors are asked to forget information they have already heard. Empirical findings suggest that they have difficulty doing so. (See Tanford, 69 Neb. L. Rev. 72 (1990).

15. Correct ruling, though "unusual" is somewhat vague, courts typically allow it as an alternative to leading ((e.g., here, "did you notice three children on the corner?")

16. Correct ruling. The testimony gives you a chance to review how generalized premises connect circumstantial evidence to ultimate facts, or to what might be termed "factual

propositions." (See Binder & Bergman, <u>Fact Investigation</u>). In support of relevance, defense counsel would argue, "People who notice children playing on the sidewalk are likely to be driving carefully," followed by, "People who are driving carefully would be likely to notice a pedestrian in a crosswalk."

Plaintiff's counsel could, of course, adopt a different premise, arguing, "People who notice children playing on a corner are likely to be distracted while driving," and, "People who are distracted while driving are likely not to notice a pedestrian in a crosswalk."

However, the counter-generalizations go to the weight of the evidence, not to its admissibility. As long as defense counsel's premise is a reasonable one, and not outweighed by 403 considerations, the evidence is relevant. That is the meaning of the "any tendency" language in Rule 401.

17. Relevant to show memory for details.

18. Based on common knowledge, opinions about age usually allowed.

19. Irrelevant.

20. Probably a correct ruling. At least as long as the question is related in time to the MSI, counsel can ask the question. The risk, of course, is that the jury may think that counsel has evidence of drinking, but is prevented from offering it due to a "technicality."

21. Incorrect ruling. Particularly where the question relates to a character-related defect, most courts will at a minimum require that counsel have a good-faith belief (e.g., based on documentation or another witness' statement) that the fact exists.

22. (a) Illustrates the practice of many judges to rule only on the specific objection that is made. If counsel chooses the wrong ground, judge may overrule even though judge would sustain an objection on a different ground. Not all judges are this strict, however.

(b) The ruling is almost surely correct. Especially without a showing that a witness was under the influence of drugs at the MSI, evidence of addiction is irrelevant. In addition, there's no tie-in to a particular drug, so the connection between a particular drug and loss of memory or perceptual capacity has not been shown.

(c) Would you want to make this objection in front of the jury? A motion in limine would be far preferable, as it might result in no mention whatsoever of drugs. Of course, that presumes that defense counsel knows before trial that this question would be asked.

23. The ruling is likewise correct. Even though plaintiff's counsel focuses on a relevant time period, without any indication that the defendant was under the influence of drugs at the time of the accident, evidence of addiction has no probative value.

24. Leading is OK on cross. Relevant to show strong financial interest in outcome of case.

25. OK to test memory for detail.

26. Improper as argumentative.

27. Proper ruling. Many students think that "asked and answered" means that a witness can't be asked the same question twice. In reality, each attorney can develop her or his own line of testimony, and can reask a question that the other has asked. This objection does come into play when the same attorney repeatedly puts the same question to a witness. On TV, the objection is often referred to as "badgering."

28. Grant the motion and strike the last sentence. It's a gratuitous remark, not an explanation.

29. The question misquotes the witness; she never said she was "annoyed." Counsel must protect the record from these subtle changes in testimony. Otherwise, the question properly trier to juxtapose evidence with conclusion, trying to show an implausibility.

30. Assuming the foundational element of a significant Hispanic population in the area, the question is probably relevant to show bias. Some judges might require an additional showing, that Hispanics have applied for jobs; others will assume it if the population size is sufficient to make it highly probable that Hispanics applied.

Transcript 5
(State v. Pinsky)

1. Witness is competent to know his own mental state. The mental state is relevant, because substantive law makes the victim's fear a material element of the crime of armed robbery.

2. You may be concerned about how the hearsay rule might affect admissibility. Since this transcript is not intended to raise hearsay issues, be assured that the hearsay rule would not bar the evidence.
There's a lot of prejudicial effect here. The statement tells the jury that the guy is a recidivist. Of all the character evidence rules which try to carefully limit admissibility of prior misconduct.
What's the relevance? Might be offered to show the witness' ability to remember details. But this detail adds little probative value to his story. Might also be offered to show the victim's fear, but the knife may be more than sufficient on this point. (Note the defense is an alibi; D doesn't contest that the robber used a knife.) Finally, might be offered to "tell the complete story of what happened." But though the oath talks about "the whole truth," extrinsic policies often limit how much truth the trier hears.
Under 403, the judge would probably keep this out. Note that one part of a conversation may be admissible, but not the other part.

3. Overrule the objection. This is basic circumstantial evidence reasoning, McCormick's "a brick is not a wall." A creative student may point out that this identifying characteristic offers a new possibility for admissibility in # 2. After all, the more speech of the robber that the victim hears, the more believable his "Southern accent" testimony.
Makes the 403 argument a tougher one for the defense.

4. (a) The evidence is relevant. Based on everyday experience, we can reasonably infer that robbers may "case" an area in advance.

Though the defendant was seen "a couple of blocks away," the inference remains reasonable.

(b) Walking "slowly." Is this an allowable opinion? Maybe this witness walks abnormally fast, and is suggesting nefarious inferences from a person's innocent gait. But if the evidence is relevant, how else can it be verbalized? It would be left to the defense attorney to try to undermine on cross, if possible.

(c) "Pretty sure." Enough for admissibility, though if it's a close 403 question, a witness' uncertainty may tip the scale towards keeping it out.

5. Would the actual knife be relevant? Sure. Though the verbal description can suffice, the actual object demonstrates that this was a real incident, and adds persuasive luster to the verbal description. A facsimile does the latter, though not the former. Probably admissible, as long as there's no attempt to mislead the jury by claiming it's the real thing, and as long as the two objects are reasonably similar. On that point, note the witness says the real knife had a longer blade. You might pose this question: what if the actual knife had a <u>shorter</u> blade? Then the prejudicial impact of the facsimile might outweigh its probative value.

6. Improper conclusion. Witness can describe the facts (lighting, time to observe, distance, etc) for trier to draw its own conclusion.

7. Witness' degree of certainty is relevant, though empirical studies often find that positive witnesses are no more likely to be accurate than uncertain ones.

8. Proper discretionary ruling under 403. Minimal relevance, even though it's the "real thing."

9. Difficult issue. The prosecution asks us to infer that the baggie was dropped by the defendant, that the defendant is an addict, and that addicts need money more than most other people. In addition, there is a risk that the

jury will punish the defendant for being a druggie, even if they're uncertain he was the robber. On balance, should be kept out.

10. The Court should rule that the magazines are irrelevant. Defendant has not tendered an issue of his ability to handle knives. Moreover, by way of foundation, to establish relevance the prosecution would probably have to establish at a minimum that the culprit here used a knife in a particular way, that a magazine article demonstrated that usage, and that the defendant read that article. None of this is included in the offer of proof.

11. Valid ruling. There's no logical connection between the witness' supposed inability to recall time of arrival on a date when nothing happened and recall of the time of the robbery.

12. The issue is whether the 3 martinis might have affected his ability to observe 3-4 hours later. I'd let it in and trust the jury to assess its probative value.

13. Improper as argumentative.

14. Whether you'd object may depend on your confidence in the witness. Many witnesses are likely to be nervous, and may have trouble being accurate. If you do object, you'll probably emphasize that the circumstances here are too different to permit any inference to be drawn from the witness' failure to make an identification. The lighting and amount of time he had to see the robber may be very different, for example. Also, judges are often reluctant to "test" witnesses. A well-reasoned objection should be sustained.

Transcript 6
(Estate of J. Paul Giddy)

1. The question misquotes the witness; he did not say he was "certain." Thus, it may imply more certainty than the witness possesses.

2. It is generally proper for a witness to say why he or she recalls a particular event. Here, the explanation is a remark made by the witness' stockbroker. The remark is therefore not offered for its truth, and is not hearsay.

3. Proper ruling, though FRE 403 might have been a more valid basis for it. Details such as what they ate are marginally relevant to show that the evening's events are clear in the witness' mind. But as they are collateral at best, and the witness' credibility has not yet been attacked, any relevance is outweighed by time and confusion problems.

4. The ruling is correct. The statement is not hearsay because Vera is not offering it for its truth, but as circumstantial evidence of Giddy's belief. Also, it is relevant, because from a statement made a few days after the will is signed we can infer the decedent's state of mind at the critical time, when the will was signed.

5. The witness' own out-of-court statement is hearsay.

6. The hearsay ruling is correct for the reason in # 4. The relevance objection may have more force, as the judge has to infer that Giddy's state of mind remained the same for two years. But given Giddy's statement after the will was signed, a judge would probably exercise discretion to allow it. Doubts about the persistence of Giddy's beliefs would go more to weight than admissibility.

7. Improper as calling for speculation; no personal knowledge.

8. The ruling is correct; Feller's statement is hearsay because the trier has to

believe Feller's out-of-court statement that Giddy made this remark.

9. The ruling is correct. Purpose of including this is to combat a popular misconception that if you don't use a witness' exact words, it's not hearsay.

10. The proper objection is "irrelevant." The witness' belief has no bearing on the issues.

11. The standard is correct (even though in most jurisdictions, will contests are not tried to juries.)

12. The only principle meant to be illustrated is the judge's power to ask questions.

13. Court has a lot of discretion as to such issues, and this ruling would be sustained on appeal.

14. Ruling OK as to "My daughter is dead," as that goes to Giddy's state of mind. But the second statement directly asserts his state of mind, and under traditional analysis is hearsay. (admissible under "state of mind exception," but here the issue is whether or not it's hearsay.)

15. Classic non-hearsay use of statements to show possible bias by the witness.

16. Good ruling. Evasive answer, counsel can press.

17. Potential non-hearsay uses include (a) bringing out the rest of the conversation; (b) that Giddy was thinking rational thoughts about his daughter; (c) impeaches the broad scope of Huge's testimony, which was to the effect that Giddy was nuts.

18. The cross examiner probably should move to strike the witness' remarks-- no question pending, and hearsay.

Transcript 7

(<u>Keaton v. Brooks</u>)

1. You should at least see the basis of the objection- that we only know our names because somebody told us. But that's how we know most things, whether it's the color red or what a car is. If the hearsay rule were to reach this broadly, nobody could testify to anything. So mostly the rule is aimed at case-specific out of court statements.

2. Radio announcer's statement could be hearsay- the announcer is not a mechanical device like a watch, and could be wrong. But if exact time isn't critical, who cares?

3. No hearsay problem, as it's offered to prove defendant's anger & frustration, not the truth of what he said.

4. Improper leading.

5. Based on common experience, the conclusion of "anger" is probably permissible. The reference to "wild beast" should be stricken upon objection as inflammatory or an improper opinion.

6. Her fright is irrelevant, and her own out of court statement is hearsay.

7. Non-hearsay, fact of anger and threat itself, apart from truth content of statement, indicates the speaker might have been the aggressor.

8. Incorrect ruling. Subject to judicial discretion under FRE 403, counsel is normally allowed to seek the exact words used during conversations. The exact words are often important, and witnesses often don't testify to exact words unless pressed to do so. Students often think that hearsay rule permits summaries of what people have said, but not their exact words. In fact, that is irrelevant to hearsay analysis.

9. Plaintiff could offer on a non-hearsay basis to show she was being defensive and

trying to avoid a fight, not to prove the truth of her being a black belt.

10. Calls for speculation.

11. A 403 problem. Plaintiff could offer statement for non-hearsay use of showing what made witness look up. But the content of the statement carries a lot of potential prejudice. You might consider a request to the court to permit a toned-down statement (e.g., "someone yelled that there was a fight").

12. This is hearsay. She doesn't say that her memory is refreshed, but just testifies to her out of court statement.

13. Hearsay, also a leading question. Students often want to simply get witnesses to confirm their deposition testimony, but though under oath, it's hearsay.

14. Irrelevant, since identity of the actors is not an issue. To the extent it's minimally relevant, it's outweighed by prejudicial impact.

15. Admissible to show lack of bias. Many works discuss a supposed rule against bolstering credibility until it's been attacked. (See e.g., Friedman, <u>Evidence</u> 285 (1991). This is wrong- attorneys do it all the time, and this is a common example. Perhaps people confuse the rule against offering evidence of good character until character has been attacked, but character is just one way of affecting credibility.

16. Clearly a specious objection- overrule. Witness' credibility is automatically in issue, and this evidence goes to credibility.

17. Overrule. While there may be some substance to claim that information comes from her doctor, people are usually credited with knowing their own physical conditions, especially those that they can perceive directly (e.g., loss of hearing). Objection might have more force if the condition were a more subtle and wholly internal one.

18. Irrelevant.

19. Hearsay; simply defendant's out of court version, no non-hearsay use is apparent.

20. Admissible to impeach; tends to discredit her in-court testimony. Thinking of the "completeness" doctrine, you may think about getting in the statement in # 19 as part of the conversation. But the two statements are easily severed; the fact that part of a conversation is admissible does not mean the rest of it is.

21. Very discretionary area. Witness has admitted making the statement, so it's not that a plain answer is impossible to give. Rather, she wants to explain the reason for the statement (Here, probably something like "I was afraid of him and just wanted to get rid of him."). In this situation, some judges allow the witness to explain, others do not. Whatever the judge does is legally permissible.

Transcript 8
(State v. Dunne)

1. The ruling is correct, as the inferences the prosecutor wants the trier to draw are legitimate.

2. This is a wholly incorrect statement. The judge should engage in a 403 weighing process. If thereafter the judge admits the statement, the judge should probably also give the jury a "limiting instruction," admonishing the jury to use the statement only for the purpose for which it was admitted.

3. The same non-hearsay use is available here as in No. 2: from her statement the trier might infer her fear of Dunne, and from that infer that it is unlikely that she would aggressively attack him. But (a) the risk that the jury will not only use it for its truth (i.e., that Dunne did kill someone), but also (b) might not sufficiently discount the accuracy of the Nichols' statement (after all, she vaguely said only that she had <u>heard</u> this) and (c) we already have other evidence of Nichols' fear makes this statement a strong candidate for exclusion under FRE 403.

4. Inadmissible hearsay, as no non-hearsay use is apparent.

5. The statement is hearsay. It would, however, probably qualify for admission under FRE 803 (state-of-mind exception). Its relevance is that it indicates a motive for Dunne to attack Dominique.

6. If Dominique's crying is tantamount to the assertion, "Yes, Dunne made those marks on me," then the testimony should be stricken as hearsay. If you regard the crying as spontaneous and not a volitional act, then the hearsay dangers do not apply and the testimony is admissible. The term "immediately" suggests the latter, but a judge might require a further foundational showing.

7. Under FRE 801(d)(2), this is a party admission, and non-hearsay.

8. Sustain the objection. The inference the prosecutor wants drawn depends on the credibility of the declarant, so the statement is hearsay.

9. The statement is inadmissible hearsay, even though the witness is testifying to her own statement. Also, it's objectionable as an opinion without sufficient foundation.

10. Correct. This is conduct, not a testimonial assertion. (This specious objection is included for educational purposes only. Actually making it in court might earn you a weekend in the slammer.)

11. Inadmissible hearsay: the defendant's out-of-court statement, relevant for no purpose other than its truth. It does not qualify as an admission under FRE 801(d)(2), because the statement is being offered by the party who made it.

12. Incorrect ruling. As the statement is inconsistent with the witness' in-court testimony, it is admissible for impeachment. The fact that the prior statement was not made under oath means only that under FRE 801(d)(1), it is not admissible for its truth.

13. Inadmissible hearsay. The statement is not inconsistent with any testimony the witness has given, and therefore no basis exists for referring to the statement that the witness made to Ihori. The proper method is to ask the witness directly whether Nichols ever made such a statement to her. Only if she denies that Nichols made such a statement could defense counsel impeach her with the statement she made to Ihori.

14. While the question is proper, the prosecutor should object that the first statement misstates the record, or misquotes the witness. The witness testified to "some large red welts," not a "couple of red spots."

15. Inadmissible hearsay of Ms. Ihori, as the witness, "I don't remember" response provides no basis for the attempted impeachment.

Also, the question is argumentative and calls for an improper opinion.

16. Permissible impeachment, suggesting that the witness might be biased against the defendant.

17. The testimony is admissible. While Ms. Sweeney's act of pointing is the equivalent of an assertive statement, here the out-of-court statement is not admitted for its truth, but to show that the officer had probable cause to arrest Dunne. If probable cause is not an issue at the trial, this non-hearsay use is irrelevant and the answer could be stricken.

18. The testimony is relevant only if Dunne's silence is the equivalent of Dunne's statement, "I did it." But in the presence of a police officer, a criminal suspect's right to remain silent means that no inference of culpability can be drawn, so the testimony is irrelevant.

19. The court should not receive the document. Though the assertions are in writing, they remain Tobias' out-of-court statements, and therefore hearsay.

20. This is a correct statement of the law.

21. This is an incorrect ruling. Under FRE 104, the jury must be excused when foundational questioning involves the admissibility of a confession.

22. This is admissible as non-hearsay. The fact that the statement was made is itself circumstantial evidence of whether this was a custodial interrogation.

23. Good thing that this is a manual on evidence and not police procedure. The officer's statement is admissible non-hearsay. Again, the very fact that it was made is circumstantial evidence showing a lack of a custodial interrogation.

24. FRE 104 provides that the rules of evidence do not apply during foundational

hearings. Nevertheless, this question asks for information beyond the officer's personal knowledge, and even during a foundational hearing should not be permitted.

25. Correct ruling. The contents of the tape are not offered for their truth, but merely to show what words were spoken.

26. Incorrect ruling. A tape may have greater probative value than the witnesses' recollection. Also, the tone of the conversation may provide additional evidence as to whether this was a custodial interrogation.

27. This is more a matter of substantive than evidence law, but the court's ruling is probably within its discretion.

Transcript No. 9
(Palmer v. Dunbar)

1. As phrased, the question may be irrelevant. Whether Palmer was a competent employee over the 10 year period is certainly relevant to negate Dunbar's claim that she was fired for poor work performance, but this question only asks the witness to compare Palmer to the other employees. Palmer might be "one of the best," but it may be a sorry lot who are all incompetent.

2. Hearsay. The testimony cannot offered to prove Tyme's state of mind, because that's irrelevant. Its only relevance is the "fact remembered" -- that Palmer was the most valuable employee -- and for that purpose it's hearsay.

3. OK. Because of its detail, students often assume a question like this is improperly leading. In fact, if (as seems likely here) none of the details are in dispute, the question legitimately calls the witness' attention to the desired subject matter to which she is to testify.

4. All of this is admissible. First, as it's a party's statement offered against the party, it's an admission. The first sentence is non-hearsay. It's not offered to prove that Palmer is an attractive employee, but to show that Dunbar was attracted to her. Asking whether Palmer is married is also circumstantial evidence of interest in Palmer. The last portion is also an assertion of Dunbar's intent, and under Mutual Life v. Hillmon it's admissible as a hearsay exception to prove that did pursue an interest in Palmer. Olsen's reply is admissible under the "completeness" doctrine which admits both parts of conversations, and at any rate her statement is not offered for the truth that Palmer is divorced, but to show why Dunbar might pursue Palmer.

5. Though part of a conversation which has already been admitted into evidence, and though Olsen's "intent" may qualify as a hearsay exception, the statements are probably irrelevant.

6. Palmer's statement that she's upset qualifies under the hearsay exception for present state of mind. But many judges would exclude the portion about Dunbar's call as hearsay. A possibility: an "excited utterance" under Rule 803 (2)?

7. Under <u>Hillmon</u> and Rule 803 (3), all is admissible, even as to the fact that Dunbar attended such a meeting.

8. OK. Present sense impression.

9. The witness' state of mind is irrelevant; this is objectionable.

10. Dunbar's counsel should move to strike the response starting with the word "because." It is non-responsive, and quite probably irrelevant.

11. Perhaps leading, but often allowed on foundational issues. (See FRE 104 (a)).

12. Close call, the ruling is certainly within a court's discretion. "Freshness" is to some extent a conclusion that can be drawn from the existence of other facts: time between event and note, absence of intervening events, etc. Rather than take the time to go into these facts, even judges who sustain the objection will probably be satisfied with use of something other than the statutory term, "fresh."

13. See No. 12 above.

14. Incorrect statement of the standard. The judge is to make the final determination of the admissibility of the evidence under an exception to the hearsay rule.

15. Correct ruling. The requirements of FRE 803 (5) have been met, thus the statement qualifies under that hearsay exception.

16. This is an incorrect ruling. The foundation for a business record has not been laid. Most importantly, the customer is not under a business duty to make accurate reports.

17. Correct ruling. Dunbar's defense is, in part, that he fired Susan Palmer for alienating customers by making disparaging remarks about the bookstore's merchandise. Thus the customer's statement is a form of "operative conduct:" the words themselves indicate that the customer was not alienated by Palmer.

18. Deny. The statement can be read into evidence, but the document itself may not be received.

19. The question is probably improper; defense attorney should object based on "lack of foundation." There is insufficient evidence of a business practice of regularly putting notes in personnel folders. This is especially true for notes made by other employees.

20. Again, though the question may appear to be leading, it is quite proper. The questioner is allowed to call the witness' attention to the specific event that the witness is to describe.

21. The ruling is well within the judge's discretion. Especially when a question limits a witness to a description of a discrete event, this sort of open question is routinely permitted.

22. Incorrect ruling. Apart from the truth of what Palmer said, it is irrelevant whether Olsen understands why Palmer was upset.

23. Correct ruling, at least insofar as making admissible that Dunbar asked Palmer to attend the book convention with him. There is sufficient circumstantial evidence that Palmer's emotions were greatly affected by what Dunbar said, and that Palmer spoke to Olsen while she was under the stress of emotion caused by Dunbar's statements. However, the admissibility of Palmer's statement about Dunbar's activities over the preceding weeks is more problematic. Palmer may not have been under the stress of those incidents when she spoke to Olsen. Thus, the "drinks and dinner meetings" statement might be stricken.

24. Proper ruling. While it is something of a conclusion, it is grounded in everyday experience and there is no viable alternative. Describing a the facial movements constituting a wink would be impossible for most people, and wasteful of court time.

25. Sustain the objection. The trier of fact is as capable as the witness of inferring Dunbar's purpose in winking.

26. Irrelevant.

Transcript No. 10
(Palmer v. Dunbar)
Same Case as No. 9

1. Proper question. It is not leading, because it refers to testimony the witness has already given. And after a break, you may repeat a limited amount of testimony to get witness and trier back "on track."

2. Proper question. Leading, but on a preliminary matter.

3. Counsel is improperly testifying in the course of marking the exhibit. Counsel should simply identify the exhibit in a way that distinguishes it from other exhibits.

4. Correct statement of the foundational burden under FRE 104.

5. Correct ruling; the foundation is adequate.

6. Correct ruling. Once the document is in evidence, the witness can inform the trier of fact of its contents.

7. Correct ruling.

8. Probably admissible: statement of present state of mind under FRE 803 (3).

9. Though this is within the court's wide discretion, the better practice would be to accede to the request.

10. The first portion is Dunbar's admission. The second is admissible as Dunbar's "admission by silence." The judge could reasonably conclude that under the circumstances it would be reasonable to expect Dunbar to respond to Olsen's remark, and that his failure to do so implies his adoption of it.

11. This objection should be sustained, and plaintiff required to lay a further foundation.

12. The objection has potential merit, though a court might well rule that the original

is not required because it is in Dunbar's possession or is collateral. FRE 1004 (3) and (4).

13. Assuming the foundational issues in Nos. 11 and 12 are overcome, the issue is whether Dunbar's failure to respond manifests his belief in Olsen's statement. While some courts have held that failure to respond to a writing cannot constitute admission by silence, the better view is to the contrary. Under the circumstances here, the court should probably overrule this objection. Note that the fact that the note states the legal conclusion of sexual harassment is not a bar to its constituting an admission.

14. Probably an incorrect ruling. While the statement is made under the stress of excitement and "relates to" the event, the statement is conclusory and speculative and should be excluded.

15. Plaintiff's counsel should object based on FRE 403: prejudice or undue consumption of time outweighs probative value. The inference that the cross examiner would be asking the trier to draw is along the lines of, "Employers who make unwelcome sexual advances towards one female employee are more likely to make unwelcome sexual advances towards other female employees than employers who do not make such advances." The accuracy of this premise is dubious: it may well be that most harassers fixate on one particular employee. But whatever the minimal accuracy, allowing the question might necessitate a host of inquiries into reasons why Dunbar might not have made advances towards Olsen, as well as Dunbar's activities towards all other female employees. Hence, an objection under 403 is appropriate.

16. This is admissible as non-hearsay, as it goes to Dunbar's state of mind, showing a possible non-discriminatory basis for firing Palmer.

17. Defendant should move to strike everything starting with "but" as irrelevant and non-responsive. (The irrelevance comes because

the issue is not whether employees <u>objected</u> to the sales procedure, but whether they <u>complied</u> with it.)

18. Proper ruling. The force of the irrelevance objection is that what matters is what Olsen reported to Dunbar, not what employees said to Olsen.

19. Admissible evidence of Dunbar's state of mind, relevant as showing a non-discriminatory basis for firing.

20. This is probably a proper ruling. Most courts allow counsel to "refresh a witness' recollection," even if the witness has made a positive assertion.

21. Correct ruling: it is admissible for the non-hearsay use of suggesting that the witness is hostile towards Dunbar.

22. The remark suggests that the witness may be biased against Dunbar, and bias is not collateral. Tindall could testify.

23. Inadmissible hearsay. It does not qualify as an admission because it is offered by the party making the statement.

24. The testimony is relevant to show that the sales procedure was unimportant to Dunbar, and thus was only a pretext for firing Palmer.

25. The first sentence qualifies as an admission, even though it is exculpatory and not an admission of wrongdoing. The plaintiff might want to introduce it anyway, because it conflicts with Dunbar's current explanation for firing Palmer (being late, not following required sales procedure.)
The second sentence, however, concerning prior discriminatory complaints leveled against Dunbar, could be objected to by Dunbar as irrelevant and improper character evidence. The admissions exception does not completely override other evidentiary rules.

26. Incorrect statement of the burden: the proponent (here, plaintiff) has the burden of

showing that the defendant intended to manifest his belief in the assertion.

27. Correct ruling. Dunbar had already expressed his belief that he had not sexually harassed Palmer, and the speaker was a government official confronting Dunbar with an official written complaint. Under these circumstances, it would be difficult to find that Dunbar intended to manifest his belief in the truth of the assertion.

28. Though an expression of a legal opinion, this qualifies as an admission, relevant to show that Dunbar may have engaged in the conduct Palmer alleges in a belief that it should not be prohibited.

29. While this does constitute a legal conclusion, it qualifies as an admissible admission by Dunbar.

30. The first portion of the answer is admissible as Dunbar's admission: it's a statement made by an employee pertaining to a matter within the scope of employment. But the latter assertion, that "Dunbar knew it," probably does not qualify as an admission, and therefore is improper hearsay. It does not pertain to bookstore policies or procedures. Also, Harrison lacks personal knowledge of Dunbar's actual knowledge, and while this might not be a problem with a statement actually made by Dunbar, it is more of a concern with a vicarious admission.

31. Correct ruling. Obviously, Harrison's statement is not offered for its truth (that business was pretty slow") but just to help paint a complete picture of this conversation, thereby adding to its credibility.

32. The testimony qualifies either as Dunbar's admission, as it concerns a matter within Harrison's scope of employment, or admissible as a present sense impression (FRE 803 (1)). However, it is irrelevant, as it pertains to a time well after Palmer was fired, and there's no showing that Dunbar was aware of the failure to follow the procedure.

33. A double hearsay problem. Dunbar's conduct might well constitute an "admission by silence." However, we have to accept the truth of Harrison's statement to find that Dunbar made this admission, and Harrison's statement is hearsay. Thus, objectionable.

34. The question is objectionably leading. But even more importantly, it seeks an improper opinion. Despite his experience, the law considers that the witness is no more capable than the trier of drawing inferences as to why Palmer was fired.

35. Inadmissible hearsay. It does not qualify as Dunbar's admission, because it is being offered by Dunbar.

36. As churning involves a propensity to be untruthful, the court has discretion under FRE 608(b) to permit this question (assuming that the questioner has a good-faith belief that the information is correct).

37. Deny. FRE 608(b) provides that the questioner must "take the witness' answer.

Transcript No. 11
(State v. Milhouse)

1. Leading; assumes a fact not in evidence. The defense is mistaken identity, yet the question assumes that the defendant was the culprit.

2. Improper compound question.

3. Leading, but OK since in the nature of cross, even though it's voir dire.

4. Correct statement of the standard, FRE 104(b).

5. Correct ruling. There is sufficient circumstantial evidence to meet the minimal 104(b) threshold.

6. The clerk's statement is admissible non-hearsay, offered to prove what called Bedoya's attention to the fact that a robbery was taking place. The defendant's statement is also non-hearsay; the words are indicative of a robbery. Alternatively, they constitute an admission. However, defendant should request that the remark about nine prior stickups be stricken. Evidence of prior robberies is inadmissible character evidence, and under FRE 403 its unduly prejudicial impact outweighs its probative value.

7. This is an erroneous statement. If an assertion is hearsay, the problem is not avoided through paraphrasing.

8. Correct ruling. The statement is relevant to show why the culprit might have killed the clerk.

9. A small point, but counsel should not "thank" the court for a favorable ruling. It implies that the judge was doing a favor rather than applying legal principles.

10. A valid opinion, based on everyday experience. Some judges might insist on a foundation that the witness has previously heard gunshots.

11. Probably admissible as an excited utterance to prove that the robber has a limp. Some judges might require more of a foundation indicating that the speaker had personal knowledge.

12. The judge has misstated the burden. Under 104(a), the burden is on the proponent of the hearsay, here, the prosecution.

13. Correct ruling in part. The nature of the injuries supports a ruling that the clerk reasonably believed death was imminent, despite the "hope to make it back" statement. The reference to a prior robbery attempt is properly stricken as improper character evidence. The "he meant to do it" assertion might also be stricken as speculative and conclusory.

14. Inadmissible hearsay.

15. Inadmissible hearsay, as there's no corroborating circumstances indicating the trustworthiness of Johnson's statement or any showing that Johnson is unavailable.

16. Admissible impeachment, as an inconsistent statement and an indication of bias.

17. Overrule the objection. "Drinking" goes to weight, not admissibility.

18. Improper legal conclusion. The officer should be asked what she said, not whether what she said constituted adequate *Miranda* warnings.

19. Again, an improper conclusion. What did he say or do?

20. Under FRE 104(d), the defendant may limit testimony to a foundational issue. However, under FRE 104(c), the hearing must be conducted out of the jury's presence.

21. Inadmissible hearsay. A "prior consistent statement," without the requirements of FRE 801(d)(1)(B) having been met.

22. A proper finding of a waiver of <u>Miranda</u> rights, but the judge's ruling is final under FRE 104 (a); the issue is not resubmitted to the jury.

23. Admissible as the defendant's admission, even though the words are exculpatory. The prosecution may want to offer it because it may conflict with the defendant's current alibi story.

24. Inadmissible. Not generally considered an "admission by silence," because a citizen, even after being <u>Mirandized</u>, needn't respond to a police officer's accusation.

25. Correct ruling. An affirmative answer suggests possible bias affecting the witness' credibility, which is implicitly in issue on direct. Therefore the question is not beyond the scope.

26. Improper impeachment under FRE 609; a specific act (excessive force) not involving the trait of trustworthiness.

27. Probably an abuse of discretion under 104 (c). Since the foundational evidence will involve threats made by the defendant, the effect of not excusing the jury is to allow improper "other crimes" evidence.

28. Probably an acceptable opinion grounded in everyday experience that would be difficult to describe in less conclusory ways.

29. The question misquotes the witness, who said only he thought it was Milhouse.

30. Correct ruling. The information is relevant for its effect on Dover's state of mind.

31. Also a correct ruling, because under FRE 104 (a) hearsay is admissible on foundational issues.

32. The foundation is probably adequate; few courts would require the witness to serve

jail time, though a short continuance might be appropriate.

33. The court should allow introduction of the preliminary hearing testimony. The factors mentioned by defense counsel might affect a judge's exercise of discretion under FRE 403, but none are bars to acceptance of the testimony. Perhaps the most important factor is the change of charge from attempted murder to murder, but given that the first charge was itself a serious one, the defense motive to impeach the testimony is similar at both the preliminary hearing and the trial.

34. By denying <u>ever</u> having robbed and shot, Milhouse may be inadvertently offering evidence of his good character under FRE (a)(1), affording the prosecution a chance to offer negative character evidence in rebuttal that it might otherwise be unable to offer on any other basis. Unless it intends to attempt to offer such rebuttal, the prosecution should object and move to strike the second sentence as non-responsive.

35. Correct ruling. The statement is not offered for its truth, but to show the reason Milhouse went to the liquor store.

36. Correct ruling. The defense is not trying to show that the witness is unavailable as foundation for the introduction of hearsay. More simply, the defense is trying to explain a potential witness' absence hoping the jury will not draw an adverse inference from the friend's failure to appear.

37. Incorrect statement of the standard. Under FRE 104 (a), the judge determines admissibility and the finding is binding on the jury.

38. Proper question, foundational, no dispute.

39. Correct ruling; under FRE 104, hearsay rule does not apply in foundational issues. In addition, there's a valid non-hearsay use: the conversation with the manager is relevant to

show the effort the investigator went to in order to try to locate the witness.

    40. Correct ruling. Under FRE 804 (a)(5), this constitutes a reasonable effort to locate the witness, especially by the defense.

    41. Probably a correct ruling. However, defendant might argue that he's entitled to bring in the whole conversation, so Cooper's statement doesn't appear to have been made in a vacuum. In that case, the prosecution would be entitled to a limiting instruction.

    42. The statement is against Cooper's interest as tending to subject him to criminal liability. But do circumstances clearly indicate the trustworthiness of the statement, as FRE 804 (b)(3) requires? The defense would point to the receipt as an indication of trustworthiness. Probably that is insufficient, unless the defense could tie the money to the robbery or negative any other source from which Cooper might have gotten the money. The statement probably would not be admissible, though an appellate court would probably not hold that a contrary ruling was an abuse of discretion.
Note that "I bet they'll cut you loose in a day or two" is not itself against Cooper's interest. Even if other parts of the statement are admitted, the prosecution should ask to have this statement excised.

    43. As an out-of-court statement consistent with the defendant's in-court testimony, the statement is inadmissible hearsay. The defense might claim that it qualifies as an "excited utterance," admissible under FRE 803 (2) regardless of unavailability. However, it is probably too conclusory to qualify for admission as an excited utterance.

Transcript No. 12
(Mentry v. McSoftware Corp.)

    1. This goes beyond allowable background into inadmissible character evidence. The trier is asked to infer that because the witness is a good citizen, she is a truth-teller.

2. Improper as assuming facts not in evidence, and calling for a narrative response.

3. Proper ruling, wrong reason. The statement isn't hearsay, but legally operative conduct: the statement constitutes breach of contract. It's also a party admission.

4. This raises a best evidence ("Original writing") problem. Possible excuses for non-production include Rule 1004(4).

5. Mentry is testifying to what Nieman told her. But given Nieman's position with the company, his statements undoubtedly constitute a party admission, and are thus non-hearsay under the FRE.
As to the content of Nieman's statement, they are probably admissible on a non-character theory under FRE 404 (b). If the only purpose of the evidence were to show that Nieman is a bad person who has a propensity to make false promises to employees of competitors, this would constitute improper character evidence. However, showing that Nieman engaged in the same or similar conduct only a year earlier suggests that Nieman did not have the intent to make an offer to Mentry this time.

6. Similar hearsay analysis as in # 5. Again there is a potential character evidence problem. If the evidence is offered simply to prove that Nieman is a thief, it is improper character evidence. Again, however, there appears to be a legitimate non-character use. Evidence that he was fired by Software King for pirating programs furnishes a motive for him to defraud Software King employees, and hence is admissible under 404(b). The defendant might request the Court to "sanitize" the statement to delete the reference to the reason that Nieman was fired, but this is unlikely to be granted.

7. This is a correct statement of the required foundational showing under FRE 104(b).

8. Correct ruling. This does not qualify for admissibility under a non-character theory. It simply shows another fraud of the defendant, and its only relevance would therefore be that

he has a propensity to engage in fraudulent conduct.

9. This is an improper statement. The witness' credibility is in issue, but not her character.

10. This ruling is correct. Evidence of the earlier incident arguably supplies a motive for the plaintiff to make up a false story about Mr. Neiman.

11. While the question may appear to be argumentative, the cross examiner is entitled to insist on an unqualified answer to the question.

12. It is a prior specific act of misconduct not amounting to a felony. Under FRE 609, the court might have discretion to admit since it does go to the witness' honesty. But the foundation here is sparse: for example, there is no showing of recency. Hence, the court should rule that this constitutes improper impeachment.

13. Assuming that defense counsel has a legitimate basis for asking the question, it is proper. Though it does suggest that Mentry has committed a criminal act, the evidence is offered not to show that she is of bad character, but that she has a motive to claim falsely that she had been hired.

14. Improper character evidence. The foundation for the witness' opinion is probably adequate. But the Federal Rules do not permit character evidence to prove conduct in civil cases.

15. Improper character evidence. The foundation for the witness to know of Nieman's reputation is probably adequate, but again, the Federal Rules do not permit character evidence to prove conduct in civil cases.

Transcript No. 13
(State v. Edwards)

1. The question assumes a fact not in evidence: that Edwards moved in with her. The relevance is also questionable, and the question is vague.

2. Improper character evidence: its only possible relevance is that the defendant has a propensity to be violent. Also, inadmissible hearsay.

3. The question is vague and/or unintelligible. An "irrelevant" objection should also be sustained.

4. Improper character evidence, suggesting that the defendant has a propensity towards violence.

5. Improper character evidence, suggesting that the defendant has a propensity to violence when using marijuana. (Note that defendant's statements are hearsay, but they would qualify as "admissions" but for the character evidence problems.)

6. Admissible evidence of "habit." Of course, to be relevant, the tune must be the one that the attacker hummed on the night of the charged attack.

7. Evidence of "habit" is generally admissible if a person repeatedly and regularly engages in certain behavior, even though less than 100% of the time.

8. Admissible as defendant's admission, relevant to connect the defendant's habit with the behavior of the attacker.

9. Judicial notice of the name of the tune would be permissible under FRE 201 (b).

10. This is a correct statement under FRE 104 (b).

11. Correct ruling; the humming would probably be sufficient to support a finding that the attacker was Edwards.

12. The court should overrule the objection. The evidence qualifies as non-character evidence under FRE 404(b), because the humming of the tune makes the evidence relevant on the issue of identity of the attacker.

13. Irrelevant; Improper character evidence; Vague. Take your pick.

14. Hearsay of Edwards, but admissible as an exception and thus relevant to prove that defendant may have committed the rape.

15. Overrule the objection. The evidence is relevant on non-character grounds. The trier might infer that the purpose of the defendant's shooting was to frighten the victim into not testifying. From that, the trier might infer that the defendant thinks that he committed a rape, and from that infer that he did commit the rape. Thus, the evidence is relevant without regard to propensity.

16. Inadmissible character evidence. Opinion evidence offered by the prosecution is admissible, if at all, only to rebut that offered by the defendant. Here, the defendant has thus far not offered evidence of character.

17. Improper character evidence. FRE 404(a)(1) allows an accused in a criminal case to offer character evidence, but the evidence must concern a trait relevant to the crime charged. Here, defendant is charged with rape, a crime of violence. Defendant's character for telling the truth is thus not a relevant character trait, and therefore inadmissible. The evidence is relevant to the defendant's credibility. But even though the defendant has testified, the defendant cannot offer character evidence in support of his credibility until the prosecution has offered character evidence to attack credibility. Since the prosecution has not done so, the evidence is not admissible on the issue of credibility.

18. Improper character evidence on two grounds: wrong character trait (see Answer # 16); because of FRE 405 (a), evidence of specific acts is not allowed under FRE 404 (a)(1).

19. As the evidence still relates to an irrelevant trait of character (see Answer # 16), this evidence too is inadmissible.

20. Admissible evidence of character under FRE 404 (a). Defendant is charged with a crime of violence, and can offer character evidence of non-violence in his own behalf.

21. Inadmissible hearsay: Catlin's out-of-court statement offered for the truth.

22. Inadmissible character evidence. Though the testimony relates to a relevant character trait, evidence of specific acts is not permitted.

23. Probably a proper ruling, as the evidence is relevant to the defendant's state of mind. If the defendant acted in accord with his intention, he would be unlikely to hang around the victim's apartment and commit a rape.

24. Estimates are generally proper, but naked guesses are not. The answer is probably objectionable and could be stricken.

25. Correct ruling.

26. Leading question, which many judges will not allow even though this portion of the testimony is foundational and FRE 104 (a) states that evidentiary rules do not apply during foundational testimony.

27. Potentially hearsay, but admissible either as indicative of the declarant's state of mind, or under FRE 104 (a) admissible because it goes to a foundational issue.

28. Probably admissible evidence of habit, though note that a picky prosecutor and/or judge might require a further foundational showing for this testimony.

29. Correct statement of the foundational burden.

30. Correct ruling.

31. Probably admissible evidence of habit, relevant to prove that Edwards went to bed by 10 P.M. the night of the rape and therefore did not attack Ms. Dalton. However, potential issues might include whether the evidence of habit is too "stale" (the witness has not lived with the defendant for a year), and whether 15-20 observations, even were that testimony admitted, enough to constitute a habit.

32. Inadmissible hearsay.

33. Improper impeachment under FRE 405. The character trait to which the question pertains (honesty) is not relevant to the admissible portion of the witness' testimony (non-violence).

34. Correct ruling. FRE 405 (a).

35. Also a proper ruling.

36. A debatable, but probably correct, ruling. The witness' opinion should pertain to the defendant's character as of the date of the incident, not to the date of trial. But most judges would not consider a 2 month difference significant enough to keep the evidence out.

37. Proper ruling. To qualify as a "good faith basis" for asking about a specific act constituting criminal misconduct, most judges require a prosecutor to have written information.

38. Deny the offer; counsel cannot offer extrinsic evidence of specific acts inquired about on cross examination of a character witness.

39. Correct ruling. The defense is not consent, but identity. Hence, whether Edwards and Dalton had previously had consensual sex is irrelevant.

Transcript No. 14
(State v. Relph)

1. The ruling is proper. Edwards' statement has a non-hearsay purpose to support Relph's claim of self-defense. If Whittington has information that Relph might be out to get him, he might take precautions against attack, and in a confrontation with Relph act as the aggressor.

2. The question is proper. Sue's statement is not hearsay, as again it goes to Whittington's belief that Relph might be violent, and lead Whittington to be the aggressor. The "barroom brawl" sounds like character evidence, but (a) it is offered by the defendant as to his own previous act of violence; and (b) it is offered not to impeach, but again to show that Whittington might have feared attack and thus decided to be the aggressor. Of course, it is tactically questionable, as it reveals Relph's violent past to the trier.

3. Proper ruling. The question does not go to Whittington's character, but to how this specific incident might have occurred.

4. Defense counsel should move to strike the last sentence as non-responsive and an improper opinion. Counsel can also ask the judge to admonish the witness to confine his answers to the question.

5. Improper character evidence. Defense counsel can try to impeach Whittington's testimony that he did not point a gun at Relph. However, counsel improperly tries to do so by suggesting that Whittington has a propensity to do so, and thus might have acted in accord with that propensity during the incident in question.

6. The question is argumentative, and before any evidence of a "criminal record" is introduced asserts an improper conclusion that it is "lamentable."

7. As improper a question as might be found in the book. Arrests are not admissible to

impeach, and the offense of indecent exposure is legally irrelevant to the trait of honesty.

8. Theft is a crime involving dishonesty, and thus admissible to impeach regardless of whether it's a felony or a misdemeanor. Three years is ordinarily recent enough to satisfy FRE 403.

9. Improper question. Only the fact of conviction is admissible, not the tawdry details.

10. The prosecutor has a right to raise the foundational issue, but cannot direct remarks directly to opposing counsel. Proper procedure is to converse "in the triangular," through the judge: "Your Honor, I request that defense counsel be ordered to indicate the source of her information."

11. The court should sustain the objection. Information based on an oral report is generally not sufficient for the "good faith basis" that one must have to impeach with a prior conviction.

12. At least two issues are involved here. First is the question of whether evidence of addiction to cocaine is admissible to impeach. On this, courts seem to be divided. The second question is whether counsel must have a good faith belief for asking the question. Especially when the question touches upon character, most courts will require that counsel's question have a basis in fact, since a jury might assume such a basis even if the witness denies being an addict. Hence, since counsel has no information suggesting that Whittington was addicted to cocaine, the question is improper.

13. and 14. The Court should overrule defense counsel's objection in No. 13. No matter what the form of the attack on the witness' character for veracity, the proponent of the witness can rehabilitate with reputation or opinion evidence of good character. However, Rule 608 makes no provision for rehabilitation with specific acts of honesty. Hence, in No. 14

defense counsel should make an objection along the following lines: "Objection, Your Honor, improper rehabilitation. Counsel is not permitted to rehabilitate with specific acts tending to prove trustworthiness."

15. A classic example of a question which though leading is proper on direct because it goes to a preliminary matter.

16. A proper ruling.

17. This is also a proper ruling, as the matter is no longer preliminary and the witness can be expected to describe her relationship with Whittington in such a way that the judge can evaluate whether the witness knows Whittington well enough to be able to express an opinion about his trustworthiness. Nos. 16 and 17 illustrate a typical difficulty counsel have: they ask a question which is extremely vague, and after an objection is sustained go completely the other way and try to repair the damage with a question that is leading and conclusory.

18. Many students are inclined to regard this as a leading question. However, unless we are to force the witness to guess which of many possible conversations counsel wants her to testify about, we must allow counsel to call the witness' attention to the desired topic. Note that opposing counsel also knows what is being asked about, allowing an objection if s/he chooses to make one. Finally, also suggesting that the question is proper is that the critical evidentiary information will have to be provided by the witness, the question does not contain it.

19. The answer raises a number of concerns:
(a) Offered to prove the fact of conviction, Whittington's statement may be hearsay. It does not qualify as an admission, since he is not a party. It is, however, inconsistent with his answer following No. 8 that he had but one conviction, and so may be admissible for impeachment purposes. In those jurisdictions in which prior inconsistent statements are admissible for their truth,

Whittington's statement would qualify as a hearsay exception.

(b) We must infer that he was convicted from his statement that he "served time." This is probably a legitimate inference. We do not know whether it was a felony conviction, but as burglary is probably a crime of dishonesty, Rule 609(a) makes the point moot.

(c) In the past, accepted ways of proving convictions were through an actual record of conviction, or the convicted person's own testimony. FRE 609(a), as amended in 1990, seemingly allows a conviction to be proven through another witness. Under Rules 403 and 611, however, the trial judge probably has discretion to exclude a prior conviction offered through another witness. Where as here the evidence is the witness' own prior statement, however, the trial judge should ordinarily allow it.

(d) The conviction is rather stale. But since the conviction is offered against a witness for the prosecution rather than against the defendant or a defense witness, the evidence should come in.

20. Is this "asked and answered?" As a general rule, counsel is not permitted to elicit the same evidence twice. (Judges often allow repetition to "rehabilitate" on redirect, or the witness has gotten confused, or there's been a time delay, etc.) However, judges occasionally allow counsel to emphasize testimony as counsel did here, throwing in a couple of additional foundation-type questions and asking if the witness is certain. A ruling either way would be appropriate, depending on the importance of the evidence, counsel's overall conduct of the trial, and the judge's temperament.

21. The first part of the question seemingly assumes a fact not in evidence, that the witness has had discussions about Whittington with co-workers.

22. This is classic reputation testimony of the type allowed by Rule 608.

23. The first sentence is classic opinion testimony of the type permitted by Rule 608.

The second sentence is debatable, although many courts allow it as simply a less abstract method of stating the opinion.

24. This is improper, as "invading the province of the jury." Even judges who might allow the second sentence in no. 23 would not allow this, as counsel tries to directly instruct the trier of fact how this specific case should be resolved.

25. This is allowable under Rule 608 (b), subject to the trial judge's discretion. As this is a very recent and very dishonest act, the better ruling would be to admit it.

26. Improper. Recognize that the difference between this and no. 25 is that here, we have to believe an out of court declarant, Sam Thompson, hence the evidence is hearsay.

27. This is not permissible impeachment, as it is not limited to the character trait of veracity. However, it would be admissible under Rule 404(a)(2), as a character trait of the victim offered by the accused.

28. Improper impeachment. It's a specific prior conduct not bearing on trustworthiness, hence under Rule 608 judge has no discretion to admit.

29. The D.A. should argue that the evidence is not being offered on the issue of the witness' character, but as evidence suggesting that she might be biased against Whittington. His reporting the bad work cost her a suspension, 3 weeks pay and her car. The evidence should be admitted on this theory, subject to judicial discretion under Rule 403. In such situations, judges sometimes consider "severing" that portion of testimony that implicates character. Here, that would be difficult. It's "all or nothing," and probably the former.

30. The Court should probably overrule the objection. Traditionally, evidence of bias is not a collateral matter, and hence counsel for the Government could offer extrinsic evidence of

the incident should Ms. Wilson deny it. As the witness is only a character witness in the first place, however, a judge might be inclined not to allow the extrinsic proof and force the Government to "take the witness' answer."

Transcript No. 15
(Matter of Kurt C.)

1. Correct ruling. The prior statement may not be admissible for its truth, but it may be admissible for impeachment purposes.

2. Correct ruling. The Federal Rules have abolished the rule in the "Queen's Case."

3. Correct ruling. The collateral evidence rule forbids <u>extrinsic</u> evidence of "unimportant" impeaching evidence, not cross examination.

4. An incorrect statement. As relevance does not depend on a disputed foundational fact, FRE 104 (b) simply does not come into play. The court should rule on the objection pursuant to FRE 403 without reference to 104 (b).

5. A correct ruling. On the relevance side, the prior statement is inconsistent. And little prejudice is likely to attach to the fact that a witness (not a party) collects unemployment; this does not implicate the witness' character.

6. Objectionable, argumentative; improper opinion.

7. Deny the request; Ms. Mertz' evidence would be collateral. Whether the witness was returning from the post office or the unemployment office is unimportant to any disputed issue.

8. A proper method of refreshing recollection.

9. Proper impeachment with a prior inconsistent statement.

10. The court should grant the request. Unlike No. 7, here the evidence would not be collateral, because evidence that the witness didn't check to see if anyone else was in the house would be important to Chaney's criminal responsibility.

11. Proper ruling under FRE 201 (b)(2).

12. Improper impeachment. This does not qualify as evidence of habit, and whether he often drinks on Friday afternoons is irrelevant to what his capacity to observe and recollect was on the date in question.

13. The reference to what Virginia said in a statement to the police is inadmissible hearsay. The statement is not inconsistent with any testimony Virginia has given, and therefore what he told the police does not qualify as a prior inconsistent statement. The questioner should simply ask whether the tub had metal legs. If Virginia says something different on the stand from what he said to the police, he can then be impeached.

14. Probably improper impeachment, because the absence of an assertion in the statement to the police that the legs were shaped like animal paws is not inconsistent with his in-court testimony. In everyday experience, this is not the sort of detail that we would expect witnesses to provide in written statements.

15. Inadmissible hearsay; improper impeachment. A witness' "I don't remember" response generally may not be impeached with a prior statement from a time when the witness did remember.

16. Calls for speculation; improper opinion.

17. Correct ruling. A cross examiner may elicit testimony that came out on direct.

18. Correct ruling; both statements are conclusory and functionally the same.

19. Correct ruling. It _is_ inconsistent for the witness to recall at a _later_ time what he could not recall at an _earlier_ time.

20. Incorrect statement; the court _does_ have discretion to strike the explanation and force opposing counsel to elicit it on redirect if opposing counsel chooses to do so. However, the court might exercise its discretion by refusing to strike the explanation in this case.

21. Improper impeachment. You cannot impeach a witness with the inconsistent statement of a different witness.

22. Proper ruling. Defense counsel would not likely be attempting to prove the truth of the statement- that Chaney receives government assistance.

23. Proper question, going to bias.

24. The ruling is partially correct: as the evidence goes to bias, it is not collateral. But as the witness has not admitted making the statement, the court should permit the extrinsic evidence.

25. No. Virginia was not asked about this statement on cross. Thus, under FRE 613 (b) defense counsel cannot offer extrinsic evidence through Mertz. Defense counsel has made no showing under that section that in interests of justice, Mertz should be allowed to testify in the absence of cross with respect to this statement.

26. Objectionable; leading. Leading questions are forbidden on redirect to the same extent as on direct.

27. Incorrect ruling. Defense counsel did not attempt to attack the witness' credibility though <u>character</u> evidence; thus the prosecution cannot offer character evidence to rehabilitate.

28. The objection probably should be sustained. Though Virginia's statement to Okla may rebut a charge that his testimony is a product of his conversation with Ms. Taten, it might well be a product of the same bias he had when he learned that Chaney received public assistance.

Transcript No. 16
(Hawthorne v. Telstar Productions)

1. Improper impeachment; irrelevant. Without more foundation, one probably cannot infer bias from the fact of non-promotion (e.g., was <u>anyone</u> promoted during that time?). If the questioner wants the trier to infer that the witness was not promoted because her work was of poor quality, that is also irrelevant.

2. Irrelevant whether it is unusual; that tells us nothing about the Hawthorne manuscript.

3. The court is correct to admonish defense counsel; "echoing" a witness' answer is an annoying habit that most judges object to. However, holding an attorney in contempt for isolated violations would be beyond the court's power.

4. Incorrect ruling. Hawthorne's character is not in issue. And since he has not testified, neither is his credibility.

5. Correct ruling. There is no showing that this witness has personal knowledge of whether Hawthorne made this statement to the receptionist, or whether any such remark is untrue.

6. Correct rulings. The remark is not offered to prove the sorry state of movies, so it is not hearsay. But to infer from it a bias against Telstar is too speculative.

7. Proper question. Goes to the witness' financial interest in the outcome: if Hawthorne wins, so does she.

8. Correct ruling; the question properly goes to the witness' motive.

9. Correct ruling. It suggests a bias in favor of Hawthorne.

10. Grant the request. It is non-responsive, and inadmissible character evidence.

11. Proper ruling.

12. Improper question. The reference to the deposition is inadmissible hearsay. It is probably also irrelevant, as from everyday experience we could not reasonably expect a person to remember the names of the manuscripts.

13. Proper question going to bias.

14. Same as # 13.

15. The ruling is within the court's proper discretion. Arguably the act of sending the letter to the paper shows greater hostility than simply writing to the Board.

16. Improper impeachment. It's vague, and not sufficient to show impairment of the witness' faculties.

17. Also improper impeachment, in the absence of any foundational evidence that this use impaired her faculties.

18. Correct ruling; preliminary matter.

19. Improper impeachment. As specific conduct not indicative of dishonesty it's improper character evidence. There's also no foundation for inferring that drug usage has impaired Sharpe's perceptual facilities. Finally, the answer is based on hearsay. All in all, a bad answer.

20. Though "good friend" is vague and rather conclusory, it's often allowed. Better practice would be, e.g., how often the people see each other socially or talk to each other.

21. Correct ruling. FRE 607 permits parties to impeach their own witnesses.

22. Correct ruling. Most courts apply FRE 613 only to prior inconsistent statements, not to other means of impeachment.

23. Incorrect statement. The evidence is admissible as long as the relevant inference is a reasonable one; it does not have to be the predominant one.

24. Incorrect ruling. The trier may choose not to infer that Sharpe's failure to mention the manuscript to a good friend was due to the fact that she never saw it, but this goes to weight, not admissibility.

25. Correct ruling. Where she took her holidays is not closely related to any important issue.

26. Ms. Sharpe's statement is admissible under FRE 803 (1) as a present sense impression.

27. Either ruling is probably within the court's discretion. The primary inconsistency concerns whether or not Sharpe examined 15 manuscripts before settling on the ones she brought with her on vacation. Since the inconsistency does concern manuscripts, a judge would most probably allow it subject to compliance with FRE 613.

28. Admissible to show personal friendship between Sharpe and the plaintiff.

29. You should respond that the statement is offered for a non-hearsay purpose: the jury may infer from the fact the remark was made that Sharpe thinks highly of Hawthorne, and from that infer that she might slant testimony in his favor.

30. Inadmissible character evidence.

31. Admissible to show possible bias in favor of the defendant.

32. The Court's ruling and remark are appropriate. Counsel is expected to show more self-control than the witness. Plaintiff counsel's proper remedy was to ask the court to strike the witness' gratuitous question.

33. Improper impeachment. Under FRE 609, a misdemeanor conviction is admissible to impeach only if it involves dishonesty.

34. Irrelevant.

35. Probably not. With no offer that the manuscript was the one by Hawthorne, the testimony would be irrelevant. Had there been a reference to Hawthorne, the impeachment would be non-collateral.

Transcript 17
(O'Hare v. Hutchinson)

1. The leading question is permissible. In effect the questioner is impeaching the witness, a tactic allowed under FRE 607. (The witness does not appear to have "forgotten," so the questioner cannot claim to be "refreshing recollection.")

2. Improper. The questioner is still attempting to impeach the witness. Though impeaching one's own witness is generally permitted, some jurisdictions forbid impeachment with prior inconsistent statements not made under oath, reasoning that to do otherwise encourages attorneys to call witnesses simply to put their prior statements before the jury in the hope that the jury will improperly accept them for their truth. But most jurisdictions would allow the impeachment, especially here where the direct seems far more than a pretext for the offering of this prior statement. However, as the questioner has offered the contents of the statement without satisfying the Original Writing Rule (Rule 1002), the attempted impeachment is improper.

3. Though an objection may be unnecessary, the witness lacks personal knowledge of the purpose for which Hutchinson ran into the store.

4. A classic example of the permissible use of a leading question to try to refresh recollection.

5. This question is more leading than the last, and perhaps even an affirmative response will be the less credible for it. But as the questioner is attempting to refresh recollection, the question is proper.

6. The Court's statement is correct. Anything shown to a witness should be marked as an exhibit, even if counsel never intends to offer it into evidence.

7. Proper ruling. Anything may be shown to a witness to refresh recollection.

8. Procedurally, counsel is supposed to remove the writing from the witness' possession before inquiring whether the witness' recollection has been refreshed, and make it clear on the record that s/he has done so.

9. Proper ruling. The witness does not appear to be testifying from present memory; she is simply referring to what's written on the report.

10. Improper statement. Plaintiff has the burden of proving that the foundation is sufficient.

11. Though conclusory, the question is proper, as accuracy is one of the foundational requirements under FRE 612. One of the stranger aspects of the hearsay exception is that while the witness no longer knows what she said, she must know that she was accurate at the time she said it.

12. The question is improper. It would be proper on cross examination, but defense counsel at this point is limited to foundational questions as to past recollection recorded.

13. Proper ruling on both grounds. Though plaintiff's counsel did not inquire into the specific event on direct, the "scope" of direct includes the freshness of Hutchinson's alleged statement in Tuvim's mind when Tuvim spoke to the officer. Information about a similar accident conveyed to Tuvim before she spoke to the officer suggests a possible lack of freshness, and thus the question is within the scope. Using the same reasoning, what the teacher told her is not hearsay-- its relevance is that regardless of whether the teacher was being accurate, information about a different accident may have made Tuvim's recollection less fresh.

14. Grant the request as to the statement from the "other witness." Whether a witness refreshes his/her recollection on the stand or before testifying, opposing counsel is entitled to see what the witness was shown. Most courts, however, would deny the request for O'Hare's

statement, on the ground that attorney-client privilege outweighs this evidentiary principle.

15. Correct ruling.

16. The question improperly assumes a fact not in evidence- that the witness told the teacher about a statement made by Hutchinson. Though FRE 104 states that evidence rules do not apply during foundation inquiries, an attorney's inserting evidence into the record is improper whenever it occurs.

17. Proper ruling. The statement of Hutchinson is an admission, and non-hearsay under FRE 801.

18. Either ruling might be proper, as a trial court has a good deal of discretion to determine "freshness." An appellate court would be unlikely to brand this ruling an abuse of discretion.

19. Improper ruling. The statement may be read into the record, but the document itself is not received.

Transcript No. 18
(Wood B. Widower v. Atlas Insurance)

1. Correct ruling.

2. The ruling is proper within the court's discretion. Defense counsel has articulated a legitimate reason for refusing the stipulation.

3. Correct ruling. As a University Professor, it's fair to assume that the witness has a string of publications; the question merely attempts to limit the answer to those that are directly relevant to the issue in this case.

4. Correct ruling. The questioner needs only to establish the witness' qualifications, not provide the trier of fact with enough information for a degree in linguistics. Also, the question is vague-- is the witness supposed to summarize each article individually? Is it likely that all are relevant to this action?

5. Assumes facts not in the record, that an appropriate term for a spectrogram is voiceprint. The answer demonstrates that the use of the term could well be misleading had the expert not clarified it on his own initiative.

6. Proper ruling. Courts generally allow far more latitude to experts, and particularly during foundational testimony.

7. Improperly leading. This testimony should come from the witness. Evidence rules do not completely disappear when an expert testifies.

8. Permissible question. A witness' having previously qualified as an expert is itself a relevant factor in the witness' expertise.

9. Proper statement; the court has discretion to permit opposing counsel to engage in foundational questioning. If the court deems the foundation inadequate, the trier of fact never hears the witness' testimony. Forcing opposing counsel to wait until cross examination

to attack foundation wastes time if the foundation is inadequate. Also, the trier of fact would then have to try to ignore testimony which it improperly heard.

10. Under FRE 104 (c), the court has discretion to conduct the foundational hearing in front of the jury. Nevertheless, the jury does not have the power to redetermine the witness' qualifications: the judge's ruling is final. Of course, the jury does have the power to <u>disbelieve</u> an expert.

11. Proper ruling.

12. The first sentence ("You testified...") is improper. Counsel is testifying instead of asking a question, even though counsel's statement pertains only to the witness' testimony. The question that follows is probably proper, as it does go to the expert's qualifications.

13. Counsel is normally permitted to cut off an explanation. If the witness or counsel calling the witness objects that an explanation is important to a full and accurate answer, the court may permit an explanation.

14. Irrelevant. This may go either to the legitimacy of the technology itself, or to Peters' credibility. Neither is at issue in this voir dire examination.

15. Proper ruling. Many items of evidence that pertain to foundation will also go to credibility, and subject to FRE 403 the court should such information during voir dire.

16. Irrelevant; the question goes to possible bias, not to Peters' qualifications. Note that the reference to the insurance company is proper, as it is a party to the action.

17. Proper ruling within the court's discretion. Notwithstanding plaintiff counsel's arguments, Dr. Peters has sufficient training and experience to qualify as an expert.

18. Proper ruling; FRE 705.

19. Proper ruling; FRE 704 (a).

20. The opinion of Dr. Tiller is inadmissible hearsay. A hearsay statement might have been admissible if the doctor used it as part of the basis of his opinion. Here, he arrived at an opinion independently of the statement, and is only testifying that another expert agrees with his opinion.

21. Proper ruling. Though linguists may for their own purposes rely in part on lay opinions, allowing them to do so in court would violate policies against unreliable hearsay.

22. Proper ruling. A court will generally permit an expert to sever off improper information if there remains an adequate basis for the expert's opinion. It's largely for the expert to say whether what remains is adequate, subject of course to dispute by an opposing expert.

23. Proper ruling, well within the court's discretion. It may be very difficult for the jurors to disregard what Bates said, but if every such problem were grounds for a mistrial many trials would never conclude. This does, however, indicate why opposing counsel should object before and not after the answer.

24. Proper ruling. A witness' confidence level, particularly that of an expert, is relevant to how much weight the trier of fact attaches to the opinion.

25. Improper question. It refers to the legal standard, which is for the trier of fact, not a witness, even an expert, to apply.

26. The ruling is within the court's discretion.

27. Improper marking process. The attorney has testified to the contents and even the probative weight ("nearly identical") of the exhibit in the guise of marking it.

28. Proper ruling. The question probably is leading, but it is foundational. Under FRE

104 (a), a leading question is proper in these circumstances.

29. Proper leading question: foundational, and asked by opposing counsel.

30. Argumentative; and no foundation for suggesting that the defense has paid a student to prepare a phony transparency.

31. The ruling that there is a sufficient showing of authenticity is proper. However, the court improperly states that it's ruling is final. Under FRE 104 (b), the jury may come to a different conclusion.

32. Proper ruling. The witness is testifying because the jury needs expert information about what inferences to draw from the spectrograms.

33. Defense counsel's statement "for the record" is permissible to enable someone reading the transcript (such as an appellate court judge) to understand the testimony.

34. Sustain the objection. Defense counsel's statement is simply repeats the witness' testimony and is not needed for clarification.

35. Proper ruling. Counsel can rebut concerns raised by an opponent as well as those that a trier of fact may itself have.

36. Though "asked and answered" is a possible objection, judges typically allow attorneys to close by emphasizing important points, even if they were covered in earlier testimony.

37. Correct ruling.

38. Incorrect ruling. The expert's failure to use other available techniques is relevant to credibility, which by definition is within the scope of direct.

39. Correct ruling; FRE 104 (a).

40. Correct ruling; the witness has stated that while he disagrees with some portions of it, he considers the report to be generally reliable. Under FRE 803 (18), that's sufficient.

41. The question improperly "assumes a fact not in evidence"- that the doctor thinks that the report is wrong about the effect of a gap.

42. Overrule the objection. Once the witness recognizes the report as authoritative, portions that call the testimony into question may usually be read into the record without giving the witness an opportunity to explain. Of course, counsel calling the expert can seek an explanation during redirect.

43. Deny the request. Under FRE 803 (18), portions may be read into the record but not received as exhibits.

44. Inadmissible hearsay. There is a hearsay opinion for statements in reliable treatises, but not for statements of other experts.

45. Correct ruling. Plaintiff's attorney is not assuming facts, but simply putting a leading question to the witness.

46. Defense counsel might object that the request is improper because the results of any such test would be irrelevant, as the test would not be conducted under laboratory conditions. Also, the results of the test might well be misleading, as listening is only the basis of a preliminary judgment which might eliminate the need for spectrographic analysis.

47. Probably improper character evidence. As a specific act involving untruthfulness, FRE 608 (b) makes cross admissible within the discretion of the court. Given the period of time which has elapsed since the incident, however, a court would be unlikely to allow it.

48. Improper impeachment. Even if the court were to allow the question in # 47, under

FRE 608 (b) the cross examiner cannot offer extrinsic evidence such as the notice.

49. Correct ruling.

50. Improper ruling. On cross counsel has leeway to ask a question more than once, particularly when the question is re-asked in a different context.

51. Improper, argumentative.

52. Overrule. As the question was argumentative, it did not call for a simple yes or no. The explanation is permissible.

53. Objectionable as leading. Leading questions are no more permissible on redirect examination than on direct.

Transcript No. 19
(In the Matter of Turney)

1. Objection, calls for a narrative response.

2. The testimony probably does not violate the Original Writing Rule (FRE 1002), as the witness is testifying to language that is <u>not</u> in the lease. See Advisory Committee's Note to Rule 1002.

3. Correct ruling. Taylor may testify to what she did without regard to the existence of a writing also pertaining to her actions.

4. Petitioner's counsel improperly "testifies" to the contents of Emall's letter. The leading question at the end is allowable under FRE 104 (a), as it is foundational.

5. Admit the exhibit; the foundation is adequate to authenticate the letter as the one sent by Emall's company. Also, the request to have it read is proper, though especially if it's lengthy some courts may deny the request and leave it for the jury to examine when the case is submitted.

6. Correct ruling.

7. Overrule the objection. Whether or not Emall had an adequate basis for making the statements, the very fact that they were made is relevant to the cause of the underlying dispute.

8. Lack of foundation for this testimony; there's no indication that the witness has personal knowledge of the amount of rent. A foundational "mini-trial" would probably show that the witness is reporting information she learned from someone else, after which the proper objection would be "hearsay."

9. The question improperly assumes facts not in evidence- that Emall did not make an effort to lease at a comparable rental price.

10. Lack or personal knowledge; speculation.

11. A leading question, but proper because it's a preliminary matter over which there is no dispute.

12. The hearsay objection should be overruled. The statement is not offered for its truth, but as the basis upon which Taylor consulted with Turney. However, the court on its own motion should strike the testimony under Rule 403. Its minimal probative value is outweighed by the potential unfair prejudice of "someone I'd have to watch carefully."

13. Irrelevant; also barred under FRE 403. A premise that attorneys whose offices are messy are more likely to urge their clients to commit perjury than those whose offices are not messy has little or no basis in experience. Also, evidence of messiness and a shot glass is likely to be unduly prejudicial. Also, "extremely messy" is an improper (vague and conclusory) opinion.

14. Question calls for an improper opinion. The witness should testify to what she said.

15. Correct ruling, wrong reason. The testimony is not hearsay because it is relevant background for understanding the scope of Turney's authority.

16. This is admissible testimony. It is relevant to the scope of the lawyer-client relationship and the advice given by Turney. It is not hearsay, both because the testimony is not offered for its truth and because any relevant statements made by Turney are admissions which come in under Rule 801 (d) (2).

17. Correct ruling. The evidence is relevant to Turney's authority and to the course of action she might have pursued.

18. "Strongly urged" is an improper opinion. The witness should testify to what Turney said and/or did.

19. Question improperly calls for speculation.

20. While the court might overrule the objection, a better ruling would be to sustain it under FRE 403. Failure to call back promptly is at best minimally connected to the charges, and may lead to undue consumption of time as Turney might seek to prove valid reasons for the delay.

21. Proper question. It is not objectionable as calling for a narrative response, as it is limited to a single conversation.

22. Proper ruling. Bashout's words are not offered for their truth. They are relevant to show why Turney might have behaved as she allegedly did.

23. The question calls for an improper legal conclusion. The witness should be asked what was said, not whether she gave "authority."

24. The statement misstates the record. The witness did not testify that she was "certain."

25. Except for the last sentence, this is a proper answer. It is relevant to explain why the memo was made, and bolsters the credibility of the witness' testimony. It is not hearsay of the business associate, because the statement is not offered for its truth. Rather, it is the basis for Taylor's actions. Opposing counsel should move to strike the last sentence as irrelevant, and ask the judge to instruct the jury to disregard it.

26. Proper. Leading but foundational (FRE 104a).

27. Admit as "present sense impression." FRE 803(1)

28. The answer should be marked as an exhibit and shown to opposing counsel before being shown to the witness. Also, the question lacks foundation- no showing that Taylor knows when the answer was filed.

29. The first sentence should be stricken; the attorney is testifying to the contents of the answer. The second sentence assumes a fact not in evidence- that Taylor noticed what the answer said.

30. The question is vague and calls for speculation as to what Turney knew.

31. The answer is objectionable: Taylor's speculation that Turney might be having drug problems is irrelevant and unfairly prejudicial.

32. Proper ruling. Exact words are relevant, and are an acceptable method of stressing important testimony.

33. Improper ruling. Under FRE 104 (a), the judge must be convinced that the witness made the declaration under the stress of excitement.

34. Even apart from the improper foundational standard, this ruling is probably wrong in part. Though a judge has a good deal of discretion, the statement "you're asking me to commit perjury," is reasonably a product of a stressful situation, is based on the witness' perception, and is largely factual. The second sentence should not be admitted, as it is a conclusion not based on perception.

35. The court is correct that another avenue of admissibility is to construe Turney's response as an adoption of Taylor's statement, but as in No. 33 the court again uses the wrong foundational standard.

36. Proper ruling, well within the court's discretion. The judge may conclude that Turney's statement amounts to an acceptance of Taylor's characterization. Even the last sentence qualifies as an admission, but Turney should ask that it be stricken as irrelevant.

37. Improper ruling. Though made under the stress of excitement, the assertion is conclusory and makes irrelevant remarks about lawyers in general.

38. Inadmissible. Though the statement constitutes an admission by Turney, it also constitutes improper character evidence. Its only relevance is to suggest that Turney has a propensity to urge perjury.

39. Proper ruling. Though a common misperception, each item of evidence need not have independent relevance.

40. Proper ruling.

41. Proper statement of the foundational standard under FRE 104(a).

42. Proper ruling. The statements are at least somewhat inconsistent. But the prior statement is not admissible for it's truth, since it was not made under oath. (Note it is not an admission, since Taylor is not a "party.")

43. You should allow it. The inference the Respondent is arguing for is reasonable, even if not iron-clad. Moreover, the issue to which the evidence relates is important, so the extrinsic evidence would not be collateral.

44. Proper ruling, within the court's discretion. Especially on cross, counsel are allowed to repeat testimony in a different context to make a point.

45. Proper ruling. The additional remarks are not necessary for an accurate answer.

46. Correct ruling. The cross examiner is simply asking a leading question.

47. Improper argumentative question.

48. Proper cross confronting the witness with the respondent's version of events. It is not argumentative, because unlike No. 47 the question makes an assertion which the witness can affirm or deny.

49. Under FRE 608(b), the court has discretion to permit counsel to ask Taylor whether she misrepresented prior ownership of a

guitar, as it is conduct going to "truthfulness" and thus relevant to credibility. However, as reference to the civil judgment is hearsay, the question is phrased improperly.

50. Deny the request. The judgment remains hearsay. In addition, the Abstract constitutes "extrinsic evidence," which is barred under FRE 608(b).

51. This is a correct statement of the rule.

52. The court correctly assigns the burden to respondent under FRE 104(a), but the correct standard is preponderance of the evidence.

53. Proper ruling. Dishonesty or false statement must be a necessary element of the crime, rather than a method by which it was committed.

54. Probably crosses the line from proper general background into being irrelevant and improper character evidence.

55. and 56. Irrelevant; improper character evidence.

57. Admissible. Without considerations of "propensity," one who teaches a professional responsibility course is less likely to violate the rules than someone who does not.

58. Correct ruling. Respondent doesn't lose her chance to tell the whole story from her perspective just because the other side goes first.

59. Overruled. The testimony is relevant for the non-hearsay purpose of proving the attorney-client relationship and the scope of Turney's authority.

60. "Nervous" is an admissible opinion based on everyday experience. The testimony is relevant as the basis of an inference that a nervous client may be somewhat more likely to suggest perjury and not accurately recall that

she authorized an answer to be filed than one who is not nervous.

61. Proper to supply details underlying the opinion; the relevance is the same as No. 60.

62. Proper ruling, incorrect reason. The testimony is non-hearsay for the reason that the words themselves are relevant to the attorney-client relationship itself and the scope of Turney's authority.

63. Overrule the objection. None of the words are offered for their truth. They are relevant to (a) rebut Taylor's version of events, and (b) as affirmative evidence that Turney acted pursuant to authority and did not advise the client to commit perjury.

64. Leading in form, but since the witness has already testified to the fact, proper for emphasis.

65. Turney's statement to Taylor is admissible non-hearsay showing that Taylor knew of the action Turney was taking on Taylor's behalf. The statement that Taylor "authorized" the filing of an answer is an improper conclusion. As earlier, Turney should testify to what was said.

66. Incorrect standard. Under FRE 104 (a) the judge determines the adequacy of the foundation.

67. Incorrect ruling. Under FRE 608 (a), this testimony would be admissible.

68. Lack of foundation for the opinion.

69. Inadmissible hearsay; improper character evidence; irrelevant. All in all, a pretty bad question.

69. Taylor's deposition statement is hearsay: it does not qualify as a "prior inconsistent statement" because it was made by a different witness. Argumentative.

70. Assuming that counsel has a good faith basis for asking the question, it is proper under FRE 404(b) to suggest that Turney might be biased against Emall and might have a motive for urging a client to commit perjury.